5ΣN

Library of
Davidson College

Indian Education Series No. 3

STUDENT POLITICS IN BOMBAY

THE UNIVERSITY OF MICHIGAN/INDIAN UNIVERSITIES
EXCHANGE PROGRAM

STUDENT POLITICS IN BOMBAY

PHILIP G. ALTBACH

ASIA PUBLISHING HOUSE
BOMBAY . CALCUTTA . NEW DELHI . MADRAS
LUCKNOW . BANGALORE . LONDON . NEW YORK

© 1968 BY THE UNIVERSITY OF MICHIGAN SCHOOL OF EDUCATION EXCHANGE PROGRAM WITH THE UNIVERSITY OF BOMBAY AND UNIVERSITY OF BARODA

SBN 210.22204.2

PRINTED IN INDIA
BY MICHAEL ANDRADES AT THE BOMBAY CHRONICLE PRESS, BOMBAY
AND PUBLISHED BY P. S. JAYASINGHE, ASIA PUBLISHING HOUSE,

FOREWORD

THIS THIRD monograph in the Indian Education Series differs from the two which preceded it—John P. Lipkin's *The Training of Secondary Teachers in Bombay* and Edward Eugene Sullivan's *Education in Social Change: A Comparison of Selected Teacher Training Colleges in Gujarat, India*—and the others scheduled to follow—studies by Donald W. Myers, Kim P. Sebaly, Peter Hackett, Richard Bennett, and Tomer L. Hogle — in that it is a dissertation submitted to the University of Chicago rather than at the University of Michigan.

It is similar to the others, however, in that part of the support for field work and travel was provided from a United States Department of State grant to the University of Michigan and in that it is published under University of Michigan auspices.

The editor of this volume was pleased to have the opportunity to counsel with the author of the study while in Bombay in 1964 and to serve with colleagues from the University of Chicago on the doctoral committee which approved the study. It is the editor's hope that this kind of co-operation may continue between Chicago and Michigan, and with other universities, and that such collaboration will lead to the production of other studies of the same high quality as the present one.

CLAUDE A. EGGERTSEN
Editor

PREFACE

MUCH OF THE discussion of the problems of higher education and student politics, in India and in other countries, has been based more on rhetoric and opinion than concrete data and thoughtful analysis. It is in the hope of providing some basic data concerning the development and current status of student activism in India that this study was undertaken. Bombay was chosen as the focus for this study because of its importance to the nationalist struggle in the pre-Independence period, and the dramatic changes which have taken place in the educational situation since 1947. It is also necessary to deal with limited areas in order to provide the detail necessary for a thorough understanding and analysis of the complex issues involved in Indian student indiscipline and activism.

The research reported here constitutes a part of the author's doctoral dissertation, and is the result of field work in India during 1964-5. This dissertation was prepared at the Comparative Education Center of the University of Chicago. Research was facilitated by the United States-Indian Comparative Education Exchange Program and the Comparative Education Center of the University of Chicago. The preparation of the material for publication was assisted by the Comparative Student Project, directed by Professor Seymour Martin Lipset, at Harvard University.

I must acknowledge the assistance and friendly criticism of my dissertation committee, Professors C. Arnold Anderson, Charles E. Bidwell, and Philip J. Foster, and to Professor Edwards Shils. Professor Claude Eggertsen of the University of Michigan and Professor Eugene Irschick of the University of California at Berkeley helped to sharpen the focus of the study.

My main debt is to the hundreds of Indian scholars, student leaders, and politicians, who gave their time and insights to this research. Without their assistance, it would have been impossible to complete this project. It is impossible to mention them all, but S. K. De of the Indian Committee for Cultural Freedom, Nurdin Karimjee of Bombay University, P. K. Kunte of the Samyukta Socialist Party, Dr. Aziz Pabany, N. R. Phatak of the Maharashtra State Committee for a History of the Freedom Movement, and Dinkar Sakrikar of *United Asia* magazine were particularly helpful. And most importantly, thanks must go to my wife, who not only did a substantial amount of the research in India, but without whose continuing encouragement and critical advice this work would have been impossible.

PHILIP G. ALTBACH

Madison
Wisconsin
January 1968

CONTENTS

Foreword — v

Preface — vii

Part I: INTRODUCTION

I STUDENTS, HIGHER EDUCATION AND POLITICS IN DEVELOPING COUNTRIES — 1
II THE STUDENT COMMUNITY AND ITS ENVIRONMENT: AN INTRODUCTION — 22

Part II: THE CONTEXT OF STUDENT LIFE: BOMBAY 1900-1965

III THE ROOTS OF STUDENT MOVEMENT (1850-1935) — 57
IV THE POLITICIZATION OF THE STUDENT MOVEMENT (1935-1942) — 73
V THE STUDENT AS POLITICAL ACTIVIST — THE 1942 MOVEMENT — 100
VI STUDENTS AND INDEPENDENCE (1943-1947) — 113
VII STUDENTS AND POLITICS SINCE 1947 — 134

Part III: ASPECTS OF STUDENTS AND POLITICS; SOME CASE STUDIES

VIII COMMUNAL STUDENT ORGANIZATIONS: THE MUSLIMS AS A CASE STUDY — 173
IX THE STUDENT PRESS IN INDIA (1930-1965) — 184
X THE TRANSITION OF THE BOMBAY STUDENT MOVEMENT — 196

Index — 213

PART I

Introduction

CHAPTER I

STUDENTS, HIGHER EDUCATION, AND POLITICS IN DEVELOPING COUNTRIES

FOR MORE than a century, student movements have had an important place among the agents of social change. In Turkey and Korea, students have been instrumental in toppling governments. In the new nations of Asia, Africa, and Latin America, students are often catalysts for political, social, and cultural development. Students have provided leadership to national liberation movements, political parties, and on a more limited scale, labor organizations and cultural groups. Not only have many of the leaders of the new states come from the ranks of the student population, but the ideological orientation of some of these societies has been influenced by student organizations and movements.

The organizational manifestation of student concern is the most dramatic indication of the power and importance of students, for it is usually the large scale student agitation which brings political results or at least captures the headlines. Whether organized by sophisticated political organisations such as the militant Zengakuren in Japan or by student groups, student demonstrations have often proven politically significant. In most new nations students often form a "potential elite". In many of these societies, students assume political responsibility even before finishing their studies, thus bringing national politics onto the campus in a very direct way. Governments are conscious of the student community, trying to influence it or perhaps repress some of its leaders. It is hard to imagine that the head of a Western nation would engage in a protracted dispute with student leaders in order to insure the loyalty of the student union. Yet, the President of the Ivory Coast recently engaged in just such a dialogue with student leaders, arguing with them, and finally threatening to suspend important government scholarships in order to insure the loyalty of the student organization. Because the government has financial and political power at its command, it can usually impose its will on the students. If all else fails, governments can, as has happened in Burma and India, close universities for extended periods. The fact that governments in many of the new nations must either argue with or force the students to accept their policies is an indication of the power of the students.

The student population in many of the developing nations is numerically small and very much out off from the rest of its peer group by vastly differing experiences, "Western" ideas, and educational opportunities. This alienation from the peer group, as well as from the mainstream of the traditional society in many cases, often makes the student community self-relient and at the same time unsure of its roots. In addition, students often have to develop their own traditions, since established patterns of "modern" educational and social behavior in many states have not as yet evolved.

Although substantial attention has been given students and higher education in the new nations, much of what has been said has been little more than uninspiring exhortation or political rhetoric. Moving beyond the cliches of the politicians and the limited proposals of educators should enable us to apply historical and sociological principles to the consideration of student political activism and higher education.

Characteristics of Students in Developing Societies

While the concept "student" has existed in the modern sense of the term since the Middle Ages, the individual student has lost much of his importance in the West in an era of mass education. In Medieval Europe, the student had something of an elite status and the accompanying freedom and prerogatives. Now, in the new nations, modern Western systems of higher education are being grafted onto traditional societies, recreating, in some aspects, older patterns of student life.

Studentship is a transitory state, usually lasting only three or four years, though perhaps extended by graduate study. While some student leaders have prolonged their affiliation to the student community, for the majority, academic life is a short, although often highly intensive period. This makes the existence of continuing organizations and sustained leadership very difficult. The problem is further aggravated by the fact that student participation in a movement is sporadic, for extracurricular activity becomes difficult to sustain when the pressure of examinations becomes intense, or for other reasons. Moreover, because the student feels he is in a period of transition, he often does not develop deep ties with the student community. Academic life is seen as a brief way station on the road to economic advancement by many, while for others it is a time of unparalleled freedom. The important differences in orientation between the generally career minded and apolitical science and professional students and the more intellectual orientation of many liberal arts students has had a number of implications. Several studies have pointed out that, in many nations, liberal arts students constitute the key element in the political movement.[1] The concept of adolescence does not exist in many traditional societies; there is simply a direct transition from childhood to adult life. The young person anticipates the freedom of his student career; however, he is often unprepared for this freedom. Relative freedom from parental and familial control, from financial responsibility (in some cases), and from outside work, combine to make the academic environment a heady experience for many. Furthermore, many realize that the student years mark the end of youth and that adult responsibilities will necessarily follow graduation from the university.

Because of their freedom, students can often afford to take risks which others in the society, saddled with family and other responsibilities, cannot take. It is partly for this reason that the student community may be considered less corrupt than any other segment of society. Student political views are supposedly unmarred by considerations of partisan politics or personal material gain. In many nations, students have taken upon themselves the leadership of the working classes and other inarticulate elements who are often unable to speak for themselves and have no tradition of organization. Students also have the reputation, perhaps justified, for having greater ideological "purity" than other elements in the society, and it is true that they can approach society without the biases of vested interests

---

[1] Metta Spencer, " Professional, Scientific, and Intellectual Students in India", *Comparative Education Review*, X, No. 2 (June 1966), p. 297.

or social constraints and a high degree of intellectual honesty. They are relatively free agents in their thought and actions, often having the security of future employment because of their education and position in the elite class.

It is no coincidence that students have often been in the vanguard of revolutionary movements in various countries. The Russian student movement provided an important impetus to revolutionary activity in the Nineteenth Century, and students in Burma, Korea, and other nations have been leading elements in independence movements. Participation in revolutionary movements if often part of the generational conflicts which are so often evident among students. Advocacy of drastic social reforms is often seen as a means of fighting the authoritarian influence of the traditional family.[2]

Because students deal with ideas and intellectualized concepts in their academic work, they are better able to understand abstract ideological systems than are persons who regularly work in more concrete situations. As a result, students are generally more receptive to ideologically oriented movements and causes. Having little or no practical experience in politics or the problems of economic development, they are often more naive about the key issues facing their societies, and are more likely to seek all-encompassing solutions to societal problems than are their elders. Because of an intellectual interest, an urge to systematize, and a psychological need to find "absolutes", students seek an ideological system which will provide them with a *Weltanschauung*, a guide to thought and action. Both left and right wing ideological movements have traditionally found strong student support, although in the developing nations the left far outweighs the right in popularity and influence.[3] This interest in intellectualized ideological systems has been an important factor in stimulating the growth of student movements and in providing them with some enduring impetus. In the non-student world, organizational initiative can help keep a movement alive. On the student

---

[2] Seymour Martin Lipset, "University Students and Politics in Underdeveloped Countries", *Minerva*, III, No. 1 (Autumn, 1964), p. 32.

[3] Glaucio A. D. Soares, "The Active Few: Student Ideology and Participation in Developing Countries", *Comparative Education Review*, X, No. 2, (June, 1966), p. 206.

level, ideological convictions among succeeding generations of students are important because of the rapidly changing nature of the student population. Organizational factors are also a key indicator of student activity. If a tradition of strong student organizational activity exists, it is much easier to sustain a movement. The organizational sophistication of the student leaders is often as important as the ideological convictions of the cadres.

In addition to the freedom which is naturally a part of student life, many societies, both traditional and advanced, have taken a permissive attitude toward student values and activity. Political acts which would be subjected to severe government repression if performed by labor unions or other groups, often go unheadded if done by students. The practice of "sowing wild oats", restricted to pranks in the United States, extends to politics in many nations, where it is assumed that students will take an active and often volatile role. This tradition of intellectual, political, and physical freedom which students enjoy in many societies acts as a reinforcing element for the student movement, permitting it to act with relative immunity.

Physiologically and psychologically, the period of adolescence is one of adjustment and change, and this cannot but have repercussions on the educational, social, and political attitudes of the students. The need for independence and self-expression are great during this period, and the tendency toward rebellion against authority, particularly that represented by the father, is marked. Studies of youth in Japan and in India indicate that many of the same factors which have been documented in the West also operate in non-Western societies.[4]

In addition to the factors which lead the individual student in a political direction, there are various constant pressures on the student population which also drive in this direction. The existence of a large number of students at one location, with similar interests and subject to similar stimuli from the environment, gives a powerful impetus for organizational activities of all kinds. It is difficult to imagine a more cohesive community from which to recruit members. The intellectual ferment which

[4] Lewis Feuer, "A Talk with the Zengakuren", *The New Leader*, XLIV, No. 18 (May 1, 1961), p. 17.

takes place as a natural result of the academic setting is also influential in moving students to action. While only a minority of any given group of students is likely to be interested in politics (or any given extra-curricular subject), the presence of substantial numbers of students in a single location tends to create a numerically significant group of committed politicized students, even though the percentages involved may remain relatively small.

Communications within the student movement are usually quite good, especially when the majority of the students in a given area are congregated on one campus. Thus, when external conditions or ideological issues move students to action, it is easy to create a substantial movement in a relatively short time. Expensive and complex newspapers, radio programs, etc., are unnecessary: all that is needed is a mimeograph machine or a few strategically placed posters. It is difficult to overestimate the value of good communications in the development of student movements. Even in totalitarian societies, these are one of the most difficult groups to control, partly because of the ease with which they can communicate among themselves.

The sense of community which is often built up by the students, due to their similarities in background and outlook and their common environment, provide a basis for a student movement or organization. Indeed, there are indications that as the student population becomes larger and less homogeneous, it is more difficult to organize large scale student movements. In India, for example, as higher education became available to young people from middle and lower middle class backgrounds and the educational institutions expanded at a rapid rate, the student community lost its cohesive quality and has been more difficult to organize.

Pressures on Students

Students have often been united by a common alienation from the traditional patterns of society. Students are often one of the few representatives of "western" culture and ideology in their societies. The structure and content of their educational institutions are largely imported and many of their teachers are either foreigners or foreign educated. There is much vacillation between traditions and modernity among students.⁵ Intellectual trends often push the students further from traditional cultural and social patterns. As a result of these factors, the students feel alienated from and superior to their families and the society at large, but at the same time they feel guilty because of their rejection of the "true" values of their culture. While the alienation often disappears as the student takes his place in society, it is an important factor during the student period.

This very sense of alienation serves to unite the student community. Alienation also has a politicizing effect, in that the values of the "modern" Western ideologies are often combined with elements of traditional culture to form the basis of new ideological movements. Elements of "African Socialism", nineteenth-century Indian revivalism, and other ideological tendencies are examples of this phenomenon. Regardless of the result of the sense of alienation, it is true that it is a powerful force on the students of the developing nations. Concepts of deracination are recurrent themes in student discussions in many of the new states. Thus, regardless of the truth in the notion, it is an important influence on student thinking, and hence on their actions.⁶

The student population also provides an organizational basis for student political and social action. Student unions and other organizations which have been set up by educational authorities or governments often provide a meeting place for students interested in discussion or cultural activity. Often, more radical groups grow out of these "official" organizations. Even in totalitarian societies, the "official" youth movements often provide the basis for dissenting groups of various kinds. Much of the impetus for the political ferment in Poland in the late Fifties, came from the Polish student movement and its publications, which were officially sanctioned by the government.⁷

Despite the fact that students in the developing nations are

⁵ Edward Shils, "Indian Students: Rather Sadhus than Philistines", *Encounter*, XVII, No. 3 (September, 1961), p. 15.
⁶ Robert Jay Lifton, "Youth and History: Individual Changes in Postwar Japan", *Daedalus*, LI, No. 1 (Winter, 1962), p. 179.
⁷ Lipset, *loc. cit.*, p. 22.

usually privileged people and have a much higher standard of living than the average citizen, the student is often under severe pressure during his academic career. Sometimes economic, but more often academic or social, these pressures help to determine the scope and intensity of student social action. The most direct pressure on the student is from the educational institution itself. The need to pass the periodic examinations, to keep up with course work, and to achieve a high academic status are some of the main worries of any student. In nations where university graduates are threatened by unemployment, and the quality of instruction is perceived by the students as inadequate, there is likely to be a good deal of underlying discontent. There is often a substantial difference in student attitudes and involvement in politics from faculty to faculty within a university. In India, for example, academic standards and employment prospects are much better for science and technological students than for those in liberal arts, and it is true that science students are not often involved in student "indiscipline". In institutions where the academic program is challenging and stimulating to the students, there is usually no problem with indiscipline.

In faculties where a good deal of ambivalence about the future and a realization that standards of education are inadequate exist, there is likely to be discontent. Academic standards and methods of university administration vary greatly in the developing nations. While some nations have worked hard to maintain educational standards and limit enrollments, others have engaged in rapid expansion of educational institutions with an accompanying lowering or standards. Educational policies imposed by governments have an important impact on students, and the nature of student organization is often determined by educational standards in various faculties, employment prospects, and other external factors.

Most traditional societies are family oriented; the individual may be primarily a member of his family rather than a citizen of the state or nation. The family can and often does apply pressure on the student. Representing the traditional values in the society, the family may influence the student towards social conformity and adherence to traditional social and religious ideas.

While the government usually exercises a rather nebulous influence on the individual student, it can on occasion become a major force in his life. Government educational policies, particularly in the developing nations, have a profound impact on the educational system, and subsequently, on the lives of individual students. Government pressure for political conformity, censorship, and suppression affect the students. Since the latter are often impatient with the slowness and ineffectuality of government of efforts in economic development, there is often opposition to the established regime. Government also represents the older generation and, in many cases, provides an obstacle to ambitious student leaders seeking quick advancement.

Politics exercise a strong attraction and potent pressure on students. Students are usually unable to match governments or well organized trade union movements in the intensity of their agitation. Yet, in many of the developing nations, political issues unrelated to education or to student affairs have caused student uprisings and agitational campaigns. Students have felt strongly enough about societal issues to sacrifie their education in order to participate in political movements and campaigns. Where active political movements exist among students, they almost always involve students intensely, consuming a great deal of time and energy.

Ideology attunes the student not only to the broader issues of his society, but makes him more willing to participate in campus-based movements. It is often true that an agitational campaign against an increase in university fees, ostensibly a campus-based issue, will be led by ideologically committed students. During the various struggles for independence and national liberation, students left the universities in substantial numbers to participate in labor movements as well as in other struggles. Ideology and political movements provide the pressure and stimulus of ideas and all-encompassing answers to some of the important questions that face the developing nations.

The environment of the individual student usually provides pressures. Indeed, much of his behavior, and his ideological views as well, are shaped by his environment. Many students suffer financial hardship during their educational careers and have to live in poor conditions. In many cases, college facilities are poor and do not provide even the basic necessities of higher education. Inadequate libraries, badly trained staff, and outmoded buildings mark many colleges in the developing nations. The impact of these conditions cannot but have an impotrant influence on the student, his attitudes, and naturally his educational attainment. Students from the working and new middle classes, whose experience with Western values is shorter and whose families can ill affort the expense of a college education, are usually affected by these factors most. The threat of unemployment hangs over the heads of many college students in the new nations, and this fear naturally has implications for the individuals involved.

Aspects of Student Political Activity

In recent years, there has been a growing realization of the importance of student activity in both educational and political development in many of the new nations.[8] Because of the fact that student political movements have had a dramatic influence in some of these nations, attention has been focused on them. It is possible to state, in capsule form, some of the general causes for student action.

It is almost a truism that the university is dependent on its environment. The student community may be aroused or swayed by events in the outside world. Political leaders often take a direct interest in students, occasionally guiding or exploiting the student movement. It has been mentioned that various national liberation movements received substantial support from students. The struggle for independence influenced the university campus and transformed many universities into battle grounds for extended periods of time. Cultural trends in the society can also have an influence on the students, as can international events, economic crises, or religious strife.

A tradition of independent political and social action and and thought among the students can help to determine the na-

---

[8] Dwaine Marvick, "African University Students: A Presumptive Elite" in James S. Coleman (ed.) *Education and Political Development* (Princeton, N. J.: Princeton University Press, 1965), p. 491.

ture and direction of the student movement. Where the student population has few traditions to fall back upon, its response to external events is unpredictable and inconsistent; where there is a tradition of apoliticism among the students, even a severe social crisis often fails to move them to action. Thus, the historical roots of the system of higher education and the student community itself both play an important part in the development of the student movement.

It is unlikely that movements stimulated by specific or isolated events will be able to sustain themselves over a long period of time. One would expect to encounter less ideological sophistication or broad political concern in them than in movements founded by politically conscious students with long range goals in mind. These "spontaneous" movements may arise when the students movements feel directly threatened or challenged. The cause can be an imposed fee increase or an unusually difficult examination. In the past, administrative censorship, suppression or condescension have instigated demonstrations in many nations. Once students have taken action on some issue, it is difficult for them to quietly return to their routine academic life after having experienced the exhilaration of political agitation and contact with the centers of powers in the society.

In the recent past, much student unrest has been collectively described as "indiscipline", as the result of immaturity or the ever-present generational conflict. While it is true that much of the violence which takes place on the campus is a result of one or the other of these factors, students have often had legitimate grievances, and are capable of expressing their concern in a disciplined and at times effective manner. They are often in the vanguard of the political and social movements of their nations and their actions frequently reflect sensitivity to social reality rather than immaturity.

Students are driven by many motives, some of them contradictory. By utilizing various methods of systematic analysis, it may be possible to discern some of the motives basic to student social and political action. Psychological examination and depth interviews will reveal facets of student behavior that an historical analysis of student activity could not, and sociologically oriented attitude surveys have much relevance. Yet, it would be a mistake to suggest that psychological and sociological methods are the only valid means of analyzing the student movement, just as a sole dependence on historical analysis would be inadequate. The social class backgrounds of the students will in part determine their attitudes toward education and occupation. Caste or tribal affiliations can also influence student attitudes. The relationship between students and society can also have an impact on the nature of the movement, since students will not tend toward political activism when there are few external causes for discontent.

There are various types of student political activity which have been important in the new states. On important distinction is the difference between norm and value oriented student political action. Norm-oriented student movements generally aim at the correction of a specific grievance or at a particular goal, and do not often have broader ideological overtones. The norm-oriented movement is unlikely to maintain itself after its goal has been attained, although such movements often provide an impetus for further activity.

While the norm-oriented movement is concerned with a specific goal and is more likely a product of an emotional response to a specific limited issue, the value-oriented movement is concerned with broader ideological issues, and when it is involved in concrete actions, these activities are usually linked directly to a broad concern.[9] Most revolutionary political movements are value-oriented, as are most on-going student political organizations, particularly "underground" groups. A value orientation does not prevent students from participating in limited campaign or agitations, although such participation is usually done for reasons transcending the specific objectives. In the student community, a value-oriented movement has a more important influence in the long run, and is often a leading element in apparently norm-oriented actions. Both types of groups, the norm-oriented "cause-group" aimed at reducing fees or securing a change in college administration, and the value-oriented political organization committed to doctrines of Marxism, Hinduism, or other ideological concepts, exist side by side in the student community. Naturally, there is some overlap

---

[9] Neil Smelser, *Theory of Collective Behavior* (New York: The Free Press, 1963), p. 275.

between these two types of groups, and it is often difficult to make a clear distinction between them, since the leadership of a group that is seemingly norm-oriented may be ideologically sophisticated and able to turn the attention of the participants to broader issues.

What starts as a limited protest against some isolated issue may easily turn into a sustained movement, with concerns extending to the broader society. The leadership of the student movement is notably fluid, and it is very possible for a norm-oriented leadership to be supplanted by students interested in capitalizing on a particular movement for broader political purposes. Thus, while norm and value orientation offer some useful models to work from, student movements often defy a tight definition of either category, and care must be taken in applying these labels to various student movements and organizations.

Student groups affiliated to political parties usually have a value orientation and are often concerned with broader political issues. Yet, it is important to keep these two sets of criteria clear, since it is possible for student movements to manifest differing orientations over a period of time. The Zengakuren, Japan's militant student organization, is clearly a value-oriented student organization, adhering to extrems leftist ideological views.[10] While its orientation has been value directed, it has switched its tactics on a number of occasions to meet the needs of the students and/or of its political ideology. The Indian student movement shows similar examples of this relatively facile change of tactics. The Communist-sponsored student organization, the All-India Students' Federation, clearly a value-oriented movement, has alternatively taken part in broader political issues under the direction of the Communist Party, and has also participated in campus-oriented activity when such action has served its needs or has become of importance to the students. It is also possible for norm-oriented student groups to take part in societal activity. At various Indian universities, students have taken part in outside politics when such action has been deemed necessary to fulfill a student demand. Pressure on political leaders can often lead to amelioration of a campus problem.

[10] Feuer, *op. cit.*, p. 17.

These distinctions are often blurred, and are hardly ever clear in the minds of the students themselves. Yet, they are a valuable tool in understanding a specific student movement. The issue is further complicated by the fact that the orientation and direction of student organizations can and often do change rather radically in a short period of time. These changes usually occur in a relatively disciplined manner, and a knowledge of the general direction of the movement can help to predict its future course.

Student political activity often contains an important non-student element, which sometimes provides direction and ideological sophistication to the movement. In most societies, the student community consists not only of students currently enrolled in institutions of higher education, but also of some ex-students or part time students who wish to remain on the periphery of the student community. While a student usually remains at an institution for four years, non-student elements in the student movement often remain for longer periods of time, providing something of an historical sense to the student movement. Political parties often assign young activists to student work and seek to expand their influence in this way. Part of the "underground" of the student population, these elements cannot be overlooked as they are often of crucial importance to student movements.

Student Movements and Organizations

Before discussing the "student movement" one must define the term. It is not a fraternity, a social club, an academic society, or an extra-curricular cultural group, although under certain circumstances it may encompass the activities and functions of such groups. We may define a student movement as an of such groups. We may define a student movement as an association of students inspired by common goals, usually, although not exclusively, political in nature. A student movement may be generated by an emotional feeling often associated with inter-generational conflicts, although motivated also by positive goals; the members of the student movement, moreover, have the conviction that, as young intellectuals, they have a special historical mission to achieve that the older generation has failed to achieve, or to correct imperfections in their environment.[11] Student movements are combinations of emotional responses and intellectual convictions.

The student movement is usually expressed in organizational terms, although not all student organizations are "movements". It is true that almost every student community has a nexus of organizations which involve individuals in various activities. These organizations exist regardless of the political composition of the student community or the form of governmental or educational authority which exists in the society. There are, furthermore, numerous types of student organizations, many of which have overlapping memberships. Groups range from large officially sponsored organizations to clandestine informal study circles.

Almost every college or university abounds with various "official" student organizations. In many institutions, officially recognized student unions are an integral part of the university community and in some places, notably Latin America, students have a constitutional voice in academic affairs. Extra-curricular social, cultural, or service organizations also involve many students. These groups provide a potentially valuable adjunct to the education of the participants, and it is common for them to be financially aided by the university administration or by the government. These groups are often formed by the university authorities for specific purposes and are subjected to strict supervision. The popularity of such groups varies, and it is a fact that many of the "official" student groups have only minimal support and participation.

In many nations, an attempt has been made to create movements on the basis of official student groups; however, such efforts have often been unsuccessful. It is also true that educational administrators or government officials frequently try to use these groups to forestall or compete with student protest organizations which oppose the authorities. Where "official" student groups have a measure of popular support, they often became a natural training and recruiting grounds for leadership. Occasionally, an official student group develops into a

[11] Lewis Feuer, "Patterns in the History of Student Movements" (mimeographed, Berkeley: University of California, 1965), p. 4.

militant student movement, sometimes opposing its patron. At different periods, the influence of these groups has varied from country to country; nevertheless, through sheer size and power, the official student organizations usually constitute an important part of the organized student community.

In addition to the official groups, most universities support a multitude of voluntary extra-curricular organizations. Although these are often recognized by university authorities and may be required to have a faculty member as an advisor, they are usually student administered. Because they have no official patronage, they stand or fall on their own merits, the average life-span of many of them is very short. These organizations range from purely social groups to those devoted to politics, social service, discussion and debate, athletics, dramatics, and culture. Many are organized by the members of a particular religious or linguistic community as a social and cultural center for their fellow members.

These organizations do not as a rule constitute movements, although they sometimes inspire more militant and massive organizational efforts. Students from a particular religious minority may, for example, in the course of discussions within an approved student group, formulate a broader religious or political creed which leads them to collaborate with or form a mass movement. Similarly, the political ideas which are discussed in such an organization can easily lead to more radical organizational activity.

Finally, there are often various kinds of unofficial and unapproved student organizations existing at a given university. Student movements are more often started by such groups than by official organizations. Such unrecognized groups are often militantly opposed to the power structure of their society. Some, however, may be of purely social nature, such as fraternities in the United States. The student "underground" may never reach an insurrectionary or active stage; yet it undeniably plays an important part in influencing its membership even at the discussion-group stage.[12]

The membership of such unapproved student groups is gene-

---

[12] Calvin Trillin, "Letter from Berkeley" in Michael Miller and Susan Gilmore (eds.), *Revolution at Berkeley* (New York: Dell Books, 1965), p. 261.

rally much smaller than the approved organizations, although this is often compensated by a high level of commitment from the membership, and a great deal of loyalty to the peer group. These associations are sometimes, but not always, affiliated to or under the influence of outside organizations, such as political parties or larger student movements. Members of highly disciplined clandestine student groups may hold high offices in "respectable" groups, thereby enhancing their influence.

All of these types of student organizations can be important in specific situations, and it would be a mistake to overlook aspects of seemingly respectable groups in any evaluation of a student movement. There is often a good deal of interaction between these various elements of the organized student population, a fact of primary importance in investigating the web of personal contacts and ideologies within the student community. The overlap of membership in various types of organizations is often substantial, and there is often an accompanying overlap of ideas. Infiltration of official student groups by the student "underground" is not uncommon and often accounts for the radical nature of ostensibly respectable organizations. The ideology of the unofficial student organizations can permeate the entire student community without much difficulty, regardless of the wishes of university officials.

A student movement need not have as its goal violent political change; it can, for example, press for a "cultural renaissance" within a society. It may also be concerned solely with educational or campus issues. Thus, in searching for the roots of a student movement or agitational campaign, it may be wise to examine all organizations, not only the militant politically motivated student groups, bearing in mind, however, that movements of a militant nature more often than not arise from ideologically committed groups.

Regardless of the type, function, or size, student groups are notoriously unstable. This is due mainly to the rapidly changing nature of the student population, but also to the changing interests of the students themselves. Even the large groups with lavish government support often lose much of their leadership and support in a short time owing to changes in the interests of the students. The clandestine organizations are still more vulnerable to changes in the winds of the student population or of society at large. It is possible, with intelligent student leadership and by careful planning and leadership training, to insure a relatively long period of organizational continuity. In the last analysis, the transitory nature of the student groups is one of their dominant characteristics and a key element in the understanding of the student community. Even seemingly stable and militant student movements can lose their popular support in a short period; internal disputes and factional disagreements can destroy the core of leadership in a matter of days, and administrative restrictions can cause serious difficulties. Other factors, such as a university examination, a diverting event in the broader society, or the arrest of key student leaders can temporarily destroy a student organization or movement. Yet it is entirely possible for a movement to recoup its losses in a very short time, thus suggesting that its ideology and program have survived a temporary organizational failure.

The Educational Role of Student Organizations

Student organizations and movements, in addition to meeting certain emotional and intellectual needs of students, also have a number of important functions within the framework of education and political development in the new nations. Student cultural and social organizations are often important sources of academic knowledge, since they sponsor well attended lectures and other programs. These organizations provide the student community with one of the few opportunities for serious discussion and a chance to meet informally with professors and other academic persons. University authorities often try to include the "extra-curriculum" as an important part of the educational experience of the students, although quite often these groups are left to the initiative of the students. In some cases, Western ideas are engendered through the activities of such group. Debating societies give valuable training in parliamentary methods, public speaking, and in politics as well. The religiously based student groups often give the students a new insight into and perhaps identification with their religious tradition. Literary groups are often as effective as formal courses in literature in providing students with a background in this field.

One of the most important educational aspects of student organizations concerns politics. Where they are permitted, most universities have active political discussion groups. Where there are constraints on student organization, such discussion groups often operate underground on a smaller scale. Discussion groups are often a primary source of political education for students and often have a vital and lasting effect on them. Student cultural organizations provide training in drama, dancing, and other arts to students who go on to become well known in the cultural realm. Students who are active in the movement often have an advantage in business and commerce because of their training in human relations and organizational techniques. Indeed, it has been said that the alumni of the militant leftist Zengakuren in Japan often make very good businessmen after their revolutionary careers come to an end.[13]

The socializing role of the student movement has been implicit in much of the foregoing discussion. Student groups are often a primary element in the political socialization of whole student generations, thereby playing an important although indirect role in the shaping of the political life of the broader society. In India, the organizational training provided by the Communist student movement has proved a valuable asset to the many former Communists who have achieved high business or government positions. Students occasionally make career choices on the basis of their experiences in the student movement, and many choose politics as a career because of their experiences in the student movement.[14]

Student organizations of all types shape student attitudes. This is a particilarly important consideration in societies in which the student community is surrounded by traditional value orientations. In such societies, the student movement is one of the few modernizing elements and can go a long way toward breaking down caste, religious, and linguistic rivalries and building a sense of nationality. Thus, social views are shaped by the student movement as well as political outlooks.

Student movements have been stimuli for nationalism in many

---

[13] Philip G. Altbach, "Japanese Students and Japanese Politics", *Comparative Education Review*, VII, No. 2 (October, 1963), p. 184.

[14] Sagar Ahluwalia, "The Student Movement in India" (unpublished paper, Delhi, 1963), p. 20.

of the new nations. Much of the modern Indian nationalism was developed by individuals with Western educations, many of whom had studied in Europe. Many of the first generation of African nationalists were trained in the London-based West African Students' Union. Student groups in other areas have also been important training centers for nationalist leaders, and some nationalistic ideology was developed within such organizations.

Conclusion

The student movement has occasionally achieved direct political results from its activities. Governments in Korea and Turkey were toppled by militant student movements, although the military soon took over the reins of government. Students in Japan forced the Kishi government to resign as a result of massive demonstrations. Students exercised an important influence on the Russian revolutionary movement and on the nationalist movements in India, Burma, and parts of Africa. Thus, the student movement can have a direct political function as well as a more diffuse educational impact. Students have never been able to successfully control a revolutionary movement, even in those instances when they have been primarily responsible for it.

The student movement is often a primary contact between the student population and the educational authorities, thus functioning as a means of communication between the two key elements in any system of higher education. Students have often taken part in educational affairs by suggesting changes and reforms which have occasionally been accepted. When students feel strongly about an educational issue, they can force the hand of the authorities by demanding reforms and enforcing their wishes by agitational campaigns.

The student movement does not always play a radical role in the community, pressing for progressive reforms and backing left-wing politicians. It can also act as a conservative force, suppporting traditional elements in the society. Although it would seem that leftism is a more pervasive influence, strong conservative student organizations exist in many nations. As in politics, the cultural influence of the student movement can be conservative as well, and can help to build an identification with traditional cultural patterns after an initial rebellion from them.

That student movements, and organizations, political and nonpolitical, have played an important and at times crucial role in the developing nations is clear. Generalizing about the nature of such movements is more difficult, since there are many differences between nations. One of the difficulties in analyzing student movements is their transitory nature—the student community as well as the interests of the students change rapidly. Organizations are often temporary, and leadership fluctuates. The emphasis of the movements shift from campus to society and back again at rather regular intervals, and the movement itself and disappear for extended periods of time.

Interaction between the educational system, the broader political and economic situation, and the socio-psychological variables of the student community is complex, making any thorough understanding of the role of students in politics and on the educational establishment difficult. Yet, it is of crucial importance that the student movement be thoroughly analyzed if an important aspect of economic and political development of the new nations is to be understood.

CHAPTER II

THE STUDENT COMMUNITY AND ITS ENVIRONMENT: AN INTRODUCTION

The Major Focus of the Study

This study has two major foci. Its first task is to describe accurately and in detail student activity and aspects of student life and of society which may have a bearing on student organizations and movements in Bombay. In this study, student activity will be defined as student attitudes, values and actions, as revealed in extra-curricular organizations and endeavors. The emphasis will be on those organizations and endeavors that have implications for student political involvement, educational attitudes and goals, and social change. The much discussed phenomenon of "student indiscipline" will be considered in its various manifestations, as will the more permanent student political, social and cultural groups.

While describing the student groups and movements that have been important during the past half century, the study will also consider educational and political conditions which have directly impinged on the activities and attitudes of the students. A mere description of student organizations without respect to their environment would not help to explain the phenomenon of student activity and the differences in such activity over a period of time. By placing student organizations in their contexts, it will be possible not only to explain better the background and causes of student activity, but also to understand more adequately higher education and politics in Bombay.

India offers a particularly good opportunity to study the breadth of student activity and student political organizations and movements in particular. A long history of educational development, including colleges and universities patterned after British models, has given independent India time to modify this system to meet its own need. With a college and university student population of one and a half million, the university has become a major institution in the society, with a vital role in the economic, social and political development of the nation. India, moreover, exhibits many of the classic problems and challenges of economic, social and political development. Agricultural modernization, industrial development, and the necessity to build a nation from many diverse elements, are all key factors in modern India.

Indian students have a long history of organized activity and political participation, dating to the beginning of the present century. Large organizations and movements first appeared in 1920. The scope and variety of Indian student organizations, both political and non-political, makes possible a detailed analysis of student activity and political involvement in a developing nation.

While India offers a unique opportunity to study student political activity and student organizations, it is much too large a nation, both in terms of population and because of differing regional patterns, to consider in any single study. Indeed, the linguistic, religious, and regional differences which divide the Indian subcontinent, make a systematic analysis of any aspect of Indian life difficult and often impossible. For this reason, this study will focus on a small area, but one which can be considered to exemplify many of the problems and developments in the subcontinent as a whole. The city of Bombay has been selected for the study, as it is a relatively compact area which shows many of the characteristics of modern India. Bombay is a key commercial center and industrial city. Its student population has taken an active part in the various campaigns of the nationalist period, although political activity has decreased somewhat in recent years.

In addition to providing a factual account of student organizational activity in Bombay, this study seeks to identify the relevant factors that have helped to determine student organizational activity as well as other aspects of student life related to politics. The hypotheses which can be drawn from this presentation can be kept in mind during the study and may provide a link between diverse groups, crises, and episodes in different historical periods.

The Educational System

The changing nature of the educational system—particularly

the colleges and the University of Bombay—has a primary impact on the types of organizations which will be formed as well as changes in existing groups. The administrative structure and policies of the colleges have an important influence on which student groups may exist openly and whether the relationship between the institution and the student groups will be amicable or hostile, for college authorities may ban groups, or discourage certain types of activity. Curriculum, examinations, language medium, faculty salaries, and outside political pressure are all important parts of an educational system and affect the nature and direction of student activity.

There is a direct and complex relationship between the field of study that a student chooses and the likelihood of his becoming a political activist. Students with a highly professional orientation, studying in a technological or scientific faculty of a university or in a technical institution, seem relatively insulated from political issues, in contrast to liberal arts students, other factors, such as caste background, secondary education, etc., remaining equal.[1] Where students feel that their educational institution is providing adequate academic preparation and a well planned and stimulating program of studies, they are less disposed towards discontent. The fact that science curricula and scientific institutions are, on the average, of higher caliber than liberal arts faculties, bears out the generalization.

Might not the "intellectual" orientation and uncertain occupational goals give liberal arts students a greater interest in social or political action than their compeers in the sciences or technical areas? Higher education is now emphasizing the sciences where employment opportunities are better; this often creates resentment among arts students. Economic pressures and anxiety about employment plague arts students. Yet, even when not beset by these extra pressures, arts students still took more than their share of political initiative and responsibility.

The Economic, Social and Political condition of Indian Society

Events and trends in society are of necessity filtered through to the student. Political parties compete for student sup-

---

[1] Metta Spencer, *op. cit.*, p. 297.

port. Students are affected by political movements such as Gandhi's campaigns, as well as by ideological trends in Indian society and the world. The influence of Marxism on student groups has been substantial during certain periods, as has Hindu traditionalism.

The overall economic situation in India has repercussions on student organizations. Fluctuating employment opportunities for university graduates influence the direction and orientation of the student movement. Insecurity, resulting from poor employment prospects, can be a stimulus to student unrest; conversely, increased competition for few jobs may make the students more prudent in their actions.

The attitudes of the political parties toward student activities can affect the student organizations, as can important political events in the nation or the world. Demonstrations aimed at broader political issues can involve large numbers of students. Indeed, mass struggles have at times seriously disrupted academic life. When political parties actively seek to use the campus as a base for political activity, there is little that the university can do to resist.

The Size and Complexion of the Student Population

The regional affiliations of Bombay students are important. The Gujaratis and Maharashtrians, as the largest groups, are significant because of their importance to the city's life and their differing roles in Bombay's development. The important religious groups in the city also offer some variations. The Hindu majority may be distinguished from the substantial Muslim minority, from the small but Westernized Parsi community, and from other groups.

A distinction must be carefully drawn between caste and class, for both form attitudes and determine roles. In a cosmopolitan city such as Bombay, class is more relevant than caste—in terms of higher education and most other areas of the "modern" sector—although a high proportion of the student population is of the Brahmin caste, the highest and traditionally the best educated caste. Caste, the traditional, hereditary, endogamous, most often localized group, usually traditionally associated with one particular occupation, is often a determinant of class status even in modern India, although occupational mobility is on the increase.[2] With the expansion of educational opportunity, the proportion of students who are Brahmins has decreased somewhat in recent years.[3] Social class, which in rural India is still directly related to caste, in Bombay is also correlated with religious and regional affiliation. Higher education in India was traditionally dominated by the Westernized segment of the higher social classes and castes. Since Independence, however, education has become increasingly available to youth from lower classes, and the Indian government has given special help to students from the "depressed classes and tribes" in an effort to diffuse education more evenly throughout the population.

Caste and class affiliation also affect student attitudes and organizational participation. In Bombay, the more affluent are often involved in student groups, while the *nouveau riche* middle class and the newly-educated working class students seem not to feel sufficiently confident to assume responsible positions. Presumably, students from the lower classes have more grievances and would therefore be more militantly involved in student movements. Yet, such students are often under severe pressure to complete their studies successfully, since they are upwardly mobile. Moreover, their unfamiliarity with the higher educational system, coupled with usually inferior secondary educations, makes them less secure and less likely to take leading roles in student organizations.

The Nature of Student Leadership

The leadership of student movements and organizations is a particularly decisive variable, since student movements tend to be rather amorphous. In the student movement, where there is an absence of strong parliamentary procedures and the regular organizational structures, leadership assumes great significance. Times of political crisis seem to produce a superior strain of student leader; this is most certainly related to the

[2] For a historical discussion concerning caste and higher education in India during the nineteenth century, see Bruce McCully, *English Education and the Origins of Indian Nationalism* (New York: Columbia University Press, 1940).

[3] M. N. Srinivas, *Caste in Modern India* (New York: Asia Publishing House, 1962), p. 3.

volatility and excitement of the situation and the high prestige given to leaders during a crisis. Student leaders are usually fairly representative of the movements which they lead (with the exception of officially appointed office bearers), and a consideration of the class and caste backgrounds of the student leadership has given some indication of the composition of the movement as a whole.

Psychological factors also have an important impact on the nature of student activity. While the usefulness of the much discussed "generational conflict" may be questioned in the Indian context, there are a number of other social-psychological factors which are applicable. The relationship between the sexes in Indian higher education has given cause for much discussion in recent years.[4] Tensions accumulated by the ambivalence of this relationship and the lack of any real co-educational contacts in a system intellectually committed to such contact gives rise to student unrest. Extra-political factors may have an important impact on student unrest and on student organizations, and may be an underlying cause of an ostensibly political issue.

Different Types and Emphases of Student Organizations

The orientations of the major student organizations will help to determine the character of the entire student movement; likewise, trends on the campus and in society affect the organizations. Moreover, changes in orientation over a period reveal shifts in the direction of the movement. The quality and commitment of the leadership, their ideological perspectives, and avowed or real goals combine to influence the direction of student activism. The impact of such forces as economic trends, political unrest, etc., on specific student organizations may also help determine their effectiveness. Outside financial support may enhance organizational stability, while undue financial or political interference may destroy it.

In the previous chapter, Smelser's distinction between norm-oriented and value-oriented movements, was discussed.[5] The

---

[4] Margaret Cormack, *She Who Rides a Peacock: Indian Students and Social Change*, (Bombay: Asia Publishing House, 1961), pp. 104-118.

[5] See Smelser, *op. cit.*

kinds of student groups which function on the campus are also
key areas of analysis. Naturally, the political groups will tend
to be particularly visible, but these are not the only groups
that earn loyalty from students.

There is a direct link between the political commitment and
the level of activity of student groups and their political viewpoint. Groups with extreme views, whether on the left or the
right, tend to be more active and to have a greater commitment from their membership than groups with moderate views.[6]

While this discussion of general factors related to the students
and their political and organizational activity does not attempt
to present a "unified" theory of student movements and organizations, it may give some theoretical basis for the following
study of student activity in Bombay. There has been an attempt
to apply sociological insights into what is essentially a historical
consideration of student activity.

Bombay as a Focal Point for the Study

Bombay offers a unique opportunity to examine students and
higher education in a relatively limited and manageable setting, while presenting most of the problems in educational development common to the new nations. While the city possesses
a secure industrial and commercial base, it is faced with many
problems of economic and social development.

Western education in Bombay antedates the establishment
of the first universities in India in 1857. Almost from its inception, Bombay has been one of the main centers of higher
education in India and has been particularly active in fields
of commercial and technical education. Its university was
founded in 1857 but had fewer than ten affiliated colleges as
late as 1920. It now has graduate departments in a number
of subjects and more than fifty-five affiliated colleges. Its
student body numbers about 65,000 — an increase of almost
100 per cent in less than twenty years. There is a great disparity in the quality of Bombay's educational institutions: the
city boasts of several of India's oldest and most prestigious
liberal arts colleges as well as newer institutions which lack

[6] Soares, *loc. cit.*

adequate resources and traditions. There is a branch of the new Indian Institute of Technology in Bombay; there are also several third or fourth-rate commercial colleges. Bombay's educational system is as varied as any in India and exemplifies the difficulties as well as the accomplishments of Indian higher education.

Many of the developing nations, and India in particular, are marked by deep social cleavages which present sizable challenges and obstacles to modernization. Bombay offers a particularly interesting case study, since among its population of almost four million are most of India's religious and regional groups. Bombay, as one of India's primary commercial centers and a major industrial city, has attracted immigrants from all over the subcontinent. The city's 50,000 Parsis give it a unique flavor, and there are substantial Jewish, Christian and Sikh communities.

Bombay also reflects India's diverse regional groups. The Gujaratis, who constitute about 30 per cent of the total, have traditionally held a dominant position in the commercial life of the city. The largest community, the Maharashtrians, have a strong cultural and linguistic tradition. Smaller groups of South Indians, Bengalis, Sikhs, and others are strongly entrenched in the city. Many of these communities have established colleges and other educational institutions and have been important in the educational and cultural life of Bombay.

A Brief Summary of Education in Bombay

Primary Education

Bombay has one of the highest levels of literacy in India, and a substantial percentage of its school-age children attend school. There are several distinct types of primary schools in Bombay, a fact which has direct bearing on the college selection process. A small minority of the institutions, usually run by private agencies or trusts, but occasionally aided by government funds, conduct most of their educational programs in English. These institious base their curriculum on centrally administered examinations necessary for college entrance. Their stress is on facility in English and the subjects which are important for the vital SSC (Secondary School Certificate) Examination. The tuition at these schools is high, and their admissions policies are selective.

Not surprisingly, the majority of the students in such institutions are from upper middle or upper class backgrounds. While these English-medium private schools constitute only a small minority of the primary schools in the city, a large proportion of their students go on to college, and because of their facility in English more adequate educational background, they have a better preparation for higher education.

A large proportion of the students at such prestige colleges as Wilson, St. Xavier's, and Elphinstone attended these English-medium primary schools. The best of these institutions and administered by Christian missionaries. Like the other institutions in the city, they are overcrowded, although enrollments are limited.

The many "middle range" primary schools are those conducted by educational trusts and communal organizations. The quality of such schools varies greatly. Most of these institutions receive substantial aid from the government in addition to fees from individual students and subsidies from the sponsoring trusts or organizations. Although these schools are generally conducted in a vernacular language, students receive some instruction in English. These schools are quite popular, and most of the ethnic and linguistic communities in Bombay run at least one primary school. The large and wealthy Gujarati community has been active in educational work and its schools can be found in most Gujarati residential neighborhoods. In addition to the Gujarati schools, the various Maharashtrian castes, Muslim communities, Parsis, South Indians, Bengalis, and others, operate their own schools. Although the syllabi used by these schools, as well as all education in the state of Maharashtra, is to a large degree prescribed by the state government, and there are periodic inspection tours by government officials, there is a wide range in quality among schools. Despite state financial aid, many of the institutions are poorly endowed and suffer from lack of qualified teachers. Because these schools are conducted primarily in the vernacular languages, many of their students have an inadequate knowledge of English or Hindi when they emerge from primary school.

The Maharashtra government operates a number of primary schools directly. These schools are generally free and have the lowest status among the primary schools in Bombay. Vernacular languages are used in these schools, and the general stress is on Marathi, little effort being made to instruct the students in English.[7] This lack of emphasis on English seriously hinders the student in his transition to an academic-oriented secondary school and hampers his chances of success in college.

There is a definite status hierarchy in primary education in Bombay, and in a real sense the choice of a primary school limits career opportunities. The missionary-run English medium schools are on the top of the hierarchy. These schools do offer the best education and are, therefore, certainly the most sensible choice at present for a student interested in continuing his education. Next in the hierarchy are institutions run by communal organizations and charitable trusts. On the bottom of the hierarchy are the government administered schools.

The period of primary schooling in Bombay is generally seven years. Most students do not continue their education after their primary school career because of lack of funds or the need to obtain a job. Those who pass the all-important examinations and are financially able to enter secondary schools usually do so at the age of twelve. Although secondary education is generally not free, the Government does provide a large number of scholarships to able students and to those from "scheduled castes and tribes". As in the case of primary education, the choice of a secondary school strongly determines one's college opportunities.

Secondary Education

Secondary education in Bombay is considered a preparation for college; few students undertake an academic secondary education without having further study in mind. Not surprisingly, a large proportion of those students who enter secondary schools ultimately do not undertake further education. The

---

[7] Integration Committee for *Secondary Education, Secondary Education in a Reorganized Bombay State* (Bombay: Director, Government Printing, 1959), p. 51.

causes for this "wastage", as it is called, are complex. Many students quit when they are unable to pass the necessary external examinations given at various points in their secondary school career, or they are unable to meet the entrance requirements of the universities. Other students are unable to undertake a college education for financial or family reasons.

As is the case with primary schools, ranking of secondary schools in Bombay is quite important, having major implications for the individual student's prospects for further education. At the top of the ladder are several well established English medium missionary administered secondary schools, which have traditionally catered to the elite of the city. The academic preparation at these schools is far superior to what is available elsewhere, and probably ranks close to a middle range British secondary school or a good American high school. An emphasis is placed on the liberal arts, and a strong effort is made to follow general procedures and keep up with the standards of British secondary education, although Indian schools are often as much as a decade behind their British counterparts in terms of both curriculum and methods. English literature and European history are stressed more than Indian humanistic subjects. In recent years, there has been some shift away from a purely European-centered curriculum, and although the Indian government has stressed the importance of Indian languages, particularly Hindi, the prestige of English-medium schooling remains high, and opens the doors to lucrative jobs in both government services and private industry. A large proportion of the graduates of these "prestige" secondary institutions go on to college, and many take post-graduate degrees as well. Because there are very few scholarship available and the fees are beyond the income of poor or even lower middle class families, these institutions tend to be extremely unrepresentative of the city's population. The clean uniforms and clothes of the students and their self-confidence and westernized attitudes are in sharp contrast to other schools in Bombay.

Below the elite secondary institutions there are a variety of schools. Many of these are operated by communal or charitable trusts and most serve one particular community in Bombay. Some of these secondary institutions are quite good, and many give a substantial stress to English-medium instruction.

It is true, however, that both the social milieu of the elite schools and the superior quality of their instruction give major advantages to their students.

Despite the existence of some scholarship assistance from the government and private sources and substantial aid programs for former untouchables, secondary education is beyond the financial ability of a large majority of the populatoin of Bombay, even if adequate primary schooling were available. The class and financial barriers to education are slowly weakening, however, and growing numbers of lower middle class, and occasionally working class students, are able to undertake secondary education. Many urban parents are willing to make substantial sacrifices to assure education for at least one member of the family.

In addition to inadequate funds, insufficient staff, and other serious problems which most secondary schools face, the standard of English taught in most of the vernacular schools is not good, and the average student from these schools has a difficult time coping with his college lectures, which are generally given in English. Thus, the graduate of a vernacular secondary school is faced with the immediate problem of an inadequate knowledge of English. As will be seen later, the cleavage between the students who have attended English-medium high schools and those who attended vernacular-medium high schools is great at the college level. This cleavage is one of the most serious and harmful effects of the class differences in Indian higher education.

Externally administered examinations are required at all levels of education. One of the most important of these examinations is the matriculation examination, which is the final test before the student leaves secondary school. This test, also called the SSC examination (Secondary School Certificate) not only evaluates the student's performance after three years of secondary education, but has a direct implication on his chances of admission to a college. Each year, a substantial number of students fail this examination, in itself a cause of great frustration and some suicides.

Even in the better secondary schools, the educational program does not provide much intellectual stimulation for the brighter students, if their own testimony can be relied upon. For able students, relatively little work is necessary to prepare for the periodic examinations. There is little class discussion, and stress is placed on rote learning. Much of the students' free time is wasted in aimless leisure activities or socializing. Only a few secondary school students also hold jobs. This lack of a challenging curriculum and substantial free time is good preparation for college, where this situation is repeated. Only during the examination periods do the students study consistently, usually working under tremendous pressure. This alternation between complete unconcern and high anxiety cannot but have some impact on the habits and attitudes of the studens.

Secondary school teachers labor under a number of disadvantages, not the least of which is a very low salary scale, averaging only 250 rupees ($ 50) per month. In addition, there is a good deal of moving from school to school, for the administration is often unwilling to promote teachers (and professors on the college level), wishing to minimize the number of tenured teachers. Schools keep teachers only for a short time, relying on a glutted labor market to fill the gaps. The preparation of many high schools teachers leaves much to be desired. Moreover, the conditions under which they are forced to teach have a dehabilitating effect on most of them. In addition to inadequate physical surroundings and a lack of books and other teaching materials, the teacher is often hampered by dictatorial administrators more interested in faculty politics and the school budget than in the quality of education. It is usually impossible to make innovations in presentation because of the overriding importance of the external examinations, which are always hanging over the heads of both teachers and students.

It can be seen that secondary school preparation in Bombay gives the students an all too realistic introduction to their colleg ecareers. Secondary schooling usually lasts from three to four years in Bombay and, as has been mentioned, is conducted in a number of the languages spoken in the city; its quality ranges from fairly good by any international standards to quite poor. Like so much in India, secondary education is divided by caste and class lines and suffers from often inadequate resources and a lack of overall planning.

Higher Education—The University of Bombay

With more than 58,000 students affiliated to its colleges and departments, the University of Bombay is one of the largest institutions on the subcontinent. Founded in 1857 along with the Universities of Calcutta and Madras, Bombay University was a creation of the British. It was consciously patterned after the University of London, and its organizational and administrative structure has changed little in the past century. As envisioned by its British planners, Bombay University was an affiliating university, setting examinations and supervising colleges, and it did not offer courses directly to students. Until the 1940's, Bombay University exercised control over the colleges in the Bombay Presidency, an area with a population approaching seventy-five million. In the recent past, it has been the policy of the Indian government to limit the scope of individual universities, and Bombay University has been confied to the corporate limits of the city of Bombay, and to Goa, which was incorporated into India in 1962.

Although Bombay University has not changed basically during its century of existence, it has gradually adopted some reform measures and has attempted to meet the needs of a changing educational system and the society. The addition of postgraduate teaching departments was an important change which began in 1934. There are now about 3,800 students in its post-graduate departments. The university has, in recent years, associated itself with various research institutions in Bombay, thereby broadening its staff and offerings. Such excellent institutions as the Tata Institute for Fundamental Research, the Tata Institute of Social Science, and others have become loosely associated with Bombay University.

The administration of Bombay University is both complex and vitally important to the educational scene in Bombay. Ultimate control over the affairs of the university rests in the university senate, which has 144 members. Some of the members hold seats by virtue of their office, such as the principals of the colleges and related institutions, and the administrative officers of the university itself. Others are appointed by the Rector of the university and include several chairmen of the university departments. There are also representatives of the teaching staff of the university and its affiliated colleges. A substantial number of the senators are elected by various elements of the public. A number are elected by the various associations of alumni of the university, and the election of several is open to the public. Thus, the senate is composed of rather diverse groups. The power of the university administration over the senate is, however, substantial, since the rector of the university directly appoints a number of the members, and has strong indirect control over others, such as the college principals and the teachers, who can be subject to administrative harassment by university officials.

The senate, which meets only periodically and cannot exercise actual control over the day to day affairs of the university, leaves most of its work to the university administration and to the Syndicate. In addition to the functions given to the university administration of by its constitution, such as setting examinations, inspection of institutions, etc., it has wide discretionary powers. It can, for example, successfully interfere in the administration of the various colleges by vetoing the appointments of professors, suggesting changes in curriculum and other matters. University administrators can, and occasionally do, privately suggest various policy changes to college principals, who usually follow the suggestions of the university to avoid conflict.[8]

The head of the university is the chancellor. The office of chancellor is, however, largely ceremonial and is usually given to a prominent public official. Nehru, for example, functioned as chancellor of several Indian universities during his lifetime. In Bombay, the chancellor is usually the governor of the State of Maharashtra. The chief administrative officers of the university in whom the power resides, are the vice chancellor and the rector, and, to a more limited extent, the registrar. In Bombay University, the rector has traditionally been the executive head of the institution.

The university is not an immediate force in the day to day lives of most of the students. They realize that the university sets the examinations and has some control over policy, but it does not impinge on their normal academic routine. When

[8] See Robert Gaudino, *The Indian University* (Bombay: Popular Prakashan, 1965), for a more complete discussion of university administration.

fees are raised, however, the students direct their protests to the university administration. Similarly, when the university decided to eliminate the morning colleges, the students protested immediately to the university, bypassing their own college administrations.

Bombay University has been one of the few institutions in India which has successfully maintained its independence of political influences from the government and from pressure groups. A long tradition of political independence, combined with strong university leadership and enlightened government officials made it possible to maintain autonomy. While the government has the legal basis to intervene in the affairs of the university, and supplies the institution with a substantial proportion of its funds, it has refrained from doing so. During the recent disputes over the morning colleges, there were powerful pressure groups, within and outside the Congress party, who sought to force the government to apply pressure on the university to change its stand on this issue, but the government officials involved refused to apply direct pressure on the university.

The Colleges

Bombay's Colleges have a long history, and were among the first to be established in India by the British. Elphinstone College, was founded in 1835 as a government financed institution. Missionaries were also active in the establishment of colleges and other schools. One of India's foremost women's educational institutions, the S.N.D.T. University, was founded in 1916. Prior to 1940, higher education in Bombay was confined mainly to the upper classes, with very few opportunities for working or middle class students. Thus, the student population was relatively small and homogeneous. There were twenty-nine colleges affiliated to the University of Bombay in 1926 with 11,059 students, although it must be remembered that the university had jurisdiction over higher education in what are now the states of Maharashtra and Gujarat. It's juristiction was limited to Bombay city only after Independence. The late 1930's, and more dramatically, the period following Independence in 1947, saw a great expansion of colleges in the city of Bombay as well as in the rest of India. Educational opportunities were extended to young people of lower class and caste groups. By 1947 there were 41,829 students attending 79 colleges affiliated to the University of Bombay, with somewhat over half in the city of Bombay.[9]

The institutions of higher education in Bombay are at the plinnacle of the educational ladder. Like the lower rungs, these institutions are stratified into different levels of varying prestige and standards of instruction. There are 54 colleges in the corporate limits of Bombay. These institutions serve 58,090 students, and have been growing at an unprecedented rate since Independence.[10] The number of colleges has increased dramatically since the 1930s. Most of the newer institutions have been established in the suburbs or in newer areas. The colleges vary substantially in traditions and quality. There are the new colleges, which have virtually no traditions and which operate in modern, though spartan, buildings in the suburbs, and colleges like Wilson or Elphinstone, which antedate the founding of the university itself in 1857 and which claim stately buildings in central Bombay. Some of the poorer institutions, such as Siddharth College, function in a renovated hotel in the central business district and hold some of their classes in a converted business office. The size of the colleges ranges from a few hundred students in some to several thousand at St. Xavier's. Their financial situation also varies greatly, and many of the institutions are perpetually in financial difficuties. Other colleges, such as K.C. College in the downtown area, are well endowed and have been able to build impressive structures in recent years.

Most students commute to college from their homes in the city and its suburbs. Many students have to travel in crowded trains and buses for two hours to reach their classes. While many of the colleges provide hostels for a few students, most of those who are admitted to them are from out of the city.

[9] Ministry of Education, *Education in Universities in India, 1958-59* (New Delhi: Ministry of Education, Government of India, 1962), p. 61.
[10] United States Educational Foundation in India, *Handbook of Indian Universities* (Bombay: Allied Publishers, 1963), p. 120.

The vast majority of the student community lives off campus and has contact with the college only during class hours. One of the considerations in selecting a college is its location. The institutions located in the middle and lower middle class sections of central Bombay naturally cater to students from these socio-economic groups, while the institutions in south Bombay cater to more upper class students. The few colleges that are located near the business district attract many working class students, who, until recently, went to morning classes and held full time jobs in addition to their college work.

It is important to consider the historical development of the colleges in trying to gain an understanding of their role in the educational structure. Bombay's colleges emerged from a variety of backgrounds. In the earliest period, prior to the founding of the university in 1857, most of the schools were founded by Christian missionaries and were clearly elitist in nature. These institutions were interested in instilling modern "Western" values in the students in order to make them more open to conversion to Christianity as well as for purely academic reasons. Until the 1930's, the scope of higher education in India was extremely limited, confined mainly to the traditionally wealthy and education-conscious upper caste families. The classical liberal arts curriculum which British missionaries imported almost unchanged from England has continued to provide the heart of Indian college education.

The historical roots of the colleges remain important to the present time. Administrative structures remain almost unchanged, as does much of the curriculum. The impact of British educational thinkers of the late nineteenth century is still clearly evident in Indian education. The elitist structure of higher education which the British created was attacked by Indians, beginning in the 1920s, and steps were gradually taken to reform the colleges. The expansion of the civil service, and the rapid development of industry and commerce in India placed stresses on the colleges for more graduates.

Of the many colleges founded to meet the expanding student population, the majority have been endowed by religious and communal groups. Siddharth College, which has been mentioned earlier, was founded by the untouchable leader B. R.

Ambedkar, and is sponsored by the Peoples' Education Society, an untouchable group. The South Indian Education Society's College in north Bombay was endowed by Tamil and Telegu elements in Bombay and serves many of them. Khalsa College is run by the Sikh community, and K.C. College by the Sindhis, who emigrated from Pakistan after partition in 1947. St. Xavier's College, which is a Jesuit institution, attracts a large number of Christian students.

The Modern College—Its Significance to the Students

We will analyze several representative colleges in Bombay bay to give an understanding of the problems facing these institutions and the position of the student within his college. Among the regular colleges, the differences between the top few institutions and the rest is well established and generally agreed upon by both students and teachers. Elphinstone, St. Xavier's, and Wilson Colleges still cater to most of the upper class students in the city and have a reputation as the best in the city. A degree from these colleges has always been more valuable than a degree from one of the newer colleges. The difference in the orientation of the students is probably greater than the variations in standards of instruction in these institutions. Despite a growing influx of students from *nouveau riche* Gujarati or Sindhi families, the students at these "elite" colleges are more oriented towards the values of the pre-Independence period. There is more leisure time and the students tend to be both articulate and fluent in English. Extra-curricular life is richer, and there is more intellectual activity. Relations between males and females, while strained, are somewhat easier than at other colleges. As time goes on, however, it would seem that the distinction between these institutions and the rest of the city's colleges will grow smaller. Other colleges have improved in quality, while academic standards at the elite schools have, if anything, declined in comparison.

It is a good deal more difficult to classify the large number of colleges which stand below the well known elite institutions. They range from quite good to very poor, and since most of the institutions are of relatively recent origin, there are no well established criteria for evaluation. Generally, the colleges which were founded in the 1930's, schools such as Khalsa, Ruia and Podar, have been able to establish themselves and evolve adequate educational programs.

Case Study—A "New" College

One of the best known "new" colleges in Bombay is Siddharth College, founded in 1946 by the Peoples' Education Society, a group of progressive untouchables. Because of its relatively unselective admissions policies and its convenient location in the central business district, Siddharth College has become one of Bombay's larger educational institutions, with 1,463 students and a teaching staff of 110[11] It has been one of the key institutions pressing for the continuation of morning colleges. The building housing the college is overcrowded most of the day, with generally inadequate facilities.

Classroom facilities are chronically inadequate at Indian colleges, and Siddharth is no exception. Science laboratories are small and ill equipped. Most classrooms are badly lit and overcrowded. Research facilities are particularly lacking. The library is quite small, containing about 45,000 volumes. It is difficult to take books out of the library owing to the pressure on their use. Undergraduate students are, moreover, unable to use the main university library, which does contain a better collection. There is virtually no place to study in the college buildings, a particularly serious handicap to the many commuting students whose homelife makes quiet studying all but impossible.

The student body at Sidharth College is diverse. Since the institution was founded by untouchable leaders (the word "untouchable" is used here, although untouchability was formally outlawed by the Indian government some years ago), it has tried to cater to the needs of students from depressed classes and tribes. Although only a minority (about 40 per cent) of the student body comes from these groups, there is a strong feeling for the origins of the college. For one thing, Siddharth is one of the few institutions in India which offers instruction in Pali, the ancient Buddhist language, and there is a stress on

[11] *Ibid.*, p. 138.

the study and observance of Buddhist culture and civilization. The main reason for this emphasis is the recent mass conversion of many ex-untouchables from Hinduism to Buddhism under the leadership of the late Dr. B. R. Ambedkar.

Buddhist student societies exist in addition to the academic work done in this area. Since untouchable students may obtain special scholarship grants from both the central and state governments, the cost of a college education is not overwhelming for them. The main problem has been finding qualified untouchable students to take advantage of the scholarships and other programs which have been offered, for secondary school facilities are still limited for these groups; furthermore, many families have difficulty in paying even the modest fees which are not covered by scholarships. In recent years, the number of untouchable students has risen dramatically, and some have been successful in law, teaching, and in other fields. Nevertheless, the stigma of their status is still great, and many jobs and positions remain closed to them.[12] The ex-untouchable students constitute a particularly interesting elements in the student community. They tend to be quiet on student issues; of the twenty student extra-curricular groups at Siddharth college, scarcely any are led by ex-untouchable students. Their academic background is often inadequate, and they have difficulty in mastering English as well as their other subjects. It is likely that several more generations of emancipation will be necessary before this group can take its full place, even at its own institution.

The rest of the student body is quiet diverse. Many qualified students attend Siddharth because of its convenient location, even though it does not have the stature of some of the older colleges in the city. It is these students, mainly from Marathi and minority backgrounds, who dominate the extra-curricular life of the college. In addition to the ex-untouchable students, many students from lower middle and working class backgrounds also attend Siddharth, both because of its location and because its standards of admission are not as rigorous as at some of the other institutions. Moreover, they feel more at ease at Siddharth

---

[12] See Harold Isaacs, *India's Ex-Untouchables* (New York: Harper and Row, 1965).

than they would at a prestige college.

Until the recent abolition of the morning colleges, there was a distinct bifurcation between the students who attended the morning colleges, leaving college for their places of work by 10 A.M. and the regular day students. Morning college students did not, for the most part, take any part in the life of the college, mainly owing to lack of time and the pressure of both academic work and full time jobs. Day students, who generally attended classes from 10 A.M. to 3 P.M., depending on rather flexible schedules, were the main elements involved in extra-curricular activities. The problem of integrating part-time students into the life of the colleges in Bombay is a serious one, and it will not be changed by the recent shift from morning to evening classes for these students. A much larger proportion of working class students attended the morning classes, for ovious economic reasons, thus making contact between the various economic groups in the college even more difficult.

College administrators have always encouraged student activities of all types and have generally taken a more liberal attitude towards such activities than is usually the case in Bombay. A substantial proportion of the student body takes part in these activities, although only a small minority is involved in the day to day functioning of the various organizations. The leadership of the extra-curricular groups in the college is generally in the hands of the better students, and these are usually from middle class families, many with English-medium secondary education. There are almost no untouchable students among the leaders of the various student groups despite the fact that they constitute a substantial proportion of the student body.[13]

There are many active student groups at the college, all of which are under the patronage and supervision of the college administration, although attempts are made to permit the students the maximum amount of latitude in their avtivities. The most active groups are the various linguistic societies, particularly the Marathi and the Kannada groups.[14] Other groups

[13] Interview with Anant Kanekar, Professor of Marathi, Siddharth College, Jnauary 25, 1965.

[24] Interview with a committee of student leaders from Siddharth College, January 14, 1965.

also hold regular meetings and occasionally sponsor publications. Gujarati, Tamil, Hindi, and several other linguistic groups are active. The English Literary and Debating Society, which is one of the student associations with high status, is also quite active and is composed mostly of students with English-medium secondary educations. This group sponsors debates, dramatic productions, and occasional lectures. It has about thirty active members.

Several "wall newspapers" are issued periodically by the various student associations. In addition to most of the language groups, the Social Sciences seminar and the Mock Parliament issue small newspapers which are handlettered and placed on a wall for the students to read. Groups devoted to dance and dramatic productions are also active, and an annual social service camp sponsored by the college in a village near Bombay always attracts a large number of students who donate their time to building roads and helping the villagers. A Social Service League has helped to set up a book lending service for poorer students, in addition to helping with the annual camp.

There seems to be little political activity at the college, although members of several outside groups, such as the Vidyarthi Parishad and the Bombay Students' Union, attend the college. The general attitude toward the college administration seems to be a positive one, and there is little evidence of the hostility that is found at some institutions. The college's Student Union is given a reasonable amount of freedom by the administration, and has been able to manage student affairs fairly efficiently in recent years. There is a student union for each of the colleges which constitute Siddharth, such as the Arts and Science College, which is the most active, law, and the Commerce and Economics colleges.

Some Siddharth students took part in the various agitational campaigns which were concerned with the volatile morning college issue, since this issue had implications for Siddharth College, which had a large morning college enrollment. Interestingly enough, however, the administration of the college was also interested in preserving the morning classes, since the college obtained valuable revenue from this arrangement. This issue, however, is probably the only political question which has concerned a substantial number of Siddharth students in recent years. The level of political consciousness at the college is probably higher than at most institutions in Bombay due to the social sciences seminar and the college parliament; yet, there seems to be but little discontent and scant interest in outside political activity of any kind.

It is difficult to estimate the percentage of students who have been involved in extra-curricular activities, although the level of activity at Siddharth seems to be higher than at most of the colleges in Bombay. There are probably twenty separate student extra-curricular groups which function on a regular basis, ranging from athletic clubs to the English Literary Society. Each of these groups has at least ten active members, and many have a larger membership.

Much of the criticism of Indian education in the past decade has centered around the student-teacher relationship. Critics have stated that this relationship is often totally nonexistent. Siddharth is typical in this regard. It is well known that most Indian college teachers are ill paid and saddled with many responsibilities. In many cases, teachers with large families have to seek additional employment, leaving practically no time for class preparation. Colleges are often unwilling to grant tenure to a teacher, which would commit them to gradual raises in his salary. They prefer to have a high turnover rate and recruit new teachers regularly at low wages from the ranks of unemployed college graduates. This means that college teaching is often an insecure profession and that many teachers have no commitment to the college in which they teach. Classes are uniformly large; even "tutorial" sessions for honors students have more than twenty-five students in all but a very few institutions. The individual teacher is not allowed much leeway in his course material and preparation, for he is forced to follow the syllabus for which the students are responsible in their all important examinations. There is no need for the students to listen to individual instructors, since their entire evaluation is on the basis of the external examination.

While Siddharth college has seen no communal or linguistic animosity during its almost two decades of existence, the students are quite aware of community differences. Most friendships are made with students of the same linguistic background, with the English-medium students being more cosmopolitan in their selection of friends and associates. College life in Bombay is not as much of a melting pot as might be expected when fairly well educated young people of various communities come together on an equal basis. While most students and faculty members discount the importance of caste as a consideration in personal relationships in present day Bombay, almost everyone points to the linguistic or religious community as an important factor in friendships and social relationships.[15]

Thus, modern education has succeeded in bringing students of different communities together, although it has not diminished the importance of linguistic or religious sectarianism in the lives of the students. Students living in hostels operated by the colleges tend to have friends from a wider variety of communities than those students who live with their families while attending college. Thus, the provincialism of the students is not altered very much by their college experiences, and the much lauded goal of national integration is certainly not served by the present situation.

The colleges, particularly the newer ones, are under tremendous pressure. The increasing demands of students for admission cannot be fully met despite the present overcrowded conditions in many institutions. Special groups demand curriculum changes, or specific educational reforms. The government asks for the improvement of standards in education, while at the same time urging that room be made for all those qualified to attend college. Students resist fee increases, while rising costs must be met. The chemistry and physics faculties demand laboratory facilities, while the university prescribes new minimum standards for faculty salaries. In many colleges (Siddharth is not mong them), the Boards of Trustees add a further pressure on administrators with their demands for special consideration for certain groups of students or for the inclusion of new programs in an already overcrowded physical plant. Special problems such as the language issue continue to plague college administrators as well as political leaders. Instruction in English continues while many elements in the population demand a

---

[15] *Ibid.*

shift in medium and standards continue to fall because of changes in policy at the elementary and secondary levels. Clearly, the operation of a college in modern day India is not an easy task.

Siddharth is an example of one of the newer colleges. Yet it is one of the better quality institutions among these newer schools, due primarily to its competent staff and leadership. While somewhat representative of similar colleges, it maintains its individual identity and peculiar features.

Case Study—an "Elite" College

In contrast to Siddharth, yet only a mile away, is Elphinstone College. Founded in 1835, prior to the establishment of the University of Bombay, Elphinstone College is a government institution and continues to receive financial assistance from the government of Maharashtra, as it had from the British authorities for a century. Elphinstone is one of the traditional elite colleges in Bombay and claims a long list of eminent alumni, including the nineteenth-century social reformer, M. G. Ranade and the radical B. G. Tilak, as well as modern business, intellectual, and political leaders.

Because Elphinstone is a government run college, it has not experienced the severe financial problems of other colleges in Bombay. While the government has remained aloof from the operation of the institution, its financial support has been vital. Because it is one of the oldest educational institutions in Bombay, Elphinstone College has been able to develop and maintain academic and social traditions, a rare feat in the context of Indian higher education. Before Independence, virtually its entire student body came from the upper classes of the city. The college has not catered to one linguistic or religious group more than to others, and while its class composition has been rather limited, it has been cosmopolitan in other ways.

Elphinstone has a tradition of high caliber liberal arts preparation, and, while its science programs have become more important in recent years, the institution still retains a very good liberal arts program which is taken more seriously than at many of the other colleges in the city. A high proportion of Elphinstone graduates have continued their educations and have gone into law or economics, and many have entered politics in the past century. A large number of the alumni of the institution have continued to take an interest in its affairs, a rarity in India, and this has been an added source of financial assistance as well as moral support.

It has been noted that Elphinstone's students came almost exclusively from upper or upper middle class families in Bombay prior to Independence, and that virtually all of these students had an English-medium secondary education. The college still retains a large number of students from this background, although there has been an influx of students from *nouveau riche* families without English-medium education and without a long family tradition of Westernized ideas and habits. As a result, the college has been divided into two, sometimes hostile, camps. These newer students, who are undoubtedly quite intelligent, often have difficulty at college because of their lack of fluency in English combined with their feelings of inferiority. These newer students tend to be serious and often, by dint of hard work, do well in the examinations. They are, however, generally quiet and unassertive.

The students from the old aristocratic families of Bombay are usually quite articulate and are among the most vocal students in India. They take a lively interest in current affairs, the arts, and particularly in Western ideas and developments. Many of these students eventually find their ways into films, advertising, and higher echelons of the foreign-owned business firms and not infrequently into the civil service. They do not work too hard at their studies, but are generally able to do well in their examinations because of their fluency in English and their superior secondary education. These students are not generally politically involved and are often cynical concerning India and their own role in its development. Students from this group are cosmopolitan, and linguistic or religious differences make little difference among them. Western social patterns are followed, with the exception of dating, which is still practiced only by a tiny minority of students. These students probably constitute a minority at present day Elphinstone, although they still dominate the college. Naturally, the frustrations of this group are substantial. The adoption of many

Western social customs must necessarily be limited by Indian traditional values, causing ambivalence for many students. Their separation from the broader Indian culture, and worry about future career choices and openings also constitute sources for worry.

Broadening of the class base of the college has had the result of causing some tensions within the student body, and has certainly not built a united student community. The kind of bifurcation that exists at Elphinstone College is found not only at the high prestige colleges; the students from the traditional Westernized upper classes feel threatened by the new students, even if they do not express these feelings openly. Some newer students have taken an interest in science and may become a threat to the hegemony of the older students in this area in the very near future.

The bifurcation which exists in the student community at Elphinstone is reflected in the extra-curricular activities of the college. Almost all student organizations are dominated by the traditional upper class group. The key group, the student council of the college, is a stronghold of these elements. Similarly, the college magazine, and the literary and debating clubs are dominated by them.

Elphinstone has had a traditional pride in its debating terms. Frequent debates are held at the college, and Elphinstone often captures trophies at the various inter-collegiate debate competitions held in the city. Again, the English language debating contests are most popular, having the highest prestige. Topics of political, philosophical, or educational interest are chosen for these debates, and the proceedings are invariably chaired by a faculty member.

The general tenor of the students remains one of apathy and a sense of frustration at being unable to influence their environment. The college administration has not encouraged students to express themselves freely. There is more underlying discontent with the educational system and with the college administration at Elphinstone than at Siddharth College, even though Elphinstone's standards are superior.

As an institution, Elphinstone College faces fewer problems than most colleges. Its physical plant, while old, is adequate for its needs, and the college has resisted pressures to expand its enrollment too quickly. The institution still receives funds from the government over and above scholarship and other limited grants which all colleges receive. The college has been struggling to maintain its academic standards in the face of somewhat declining standards of secondary education, and has been trying to keep its staff at a high level. It has not been as threatened by the decline in standards of English on the secondary level, since a fairly large proportion of its students come from private English-medium secondary schools and speak English at home. The institution has had a more difficult time in attracting the best students, owing to the rise of other good quality colleges and the interest of an increasing number of talented students in technical education.

Higher Education in Bombay: Some Concluding Comments

While only two of Bombay's fifty-four liberal arts colleges have been considered in detail, they have given a picture of college life in the city. Most of the colleges are far inferior to the institutions discussed here. Recently established colleges located in the suburban areas are financially in a precarious position. Library facilities, universally inadequate in India, are almost non-existent in the suburban colleges; students must often travel long distances to reach an adequate library. It is also difficult for the suburban colleges to attract quality teachers. These colleges feel, with some justification, that they must stabilize their financial condition by attracting the maximum number of students, regardless of their qualifications, if they are to survive.

This proliferation of colleges has had major implications for higher education in Bombay. The newer colleges have inactive extra-curricular programs and are much less diverse in their student bodies. The proportion of students coming from English-medium schools is generally quite small. For the science students, laboratory facilities are often even more inadequate than they are at the older institutions.

The foundation and maintenance of an institution of higher learning has become a status symbol among linguistic and religious communities in Bombay. Groups able to afford the initial investment have founded colleges without regard to the future development of the institution. As more colleges develop in the suburbs, their educational standards will inevitably suffer, since the number of qualified secondary school graduates in that area is limited. University authorities have exercised little control over the expansion of institutions, and have confined themselves to stressing the maintenance of minimum standards of quality for the institutions once they are established.

Technical education attracts some of the best students because of its high prestige and favorable employment prospects. Because of rigorous educational programs and facilities, there is less student unrest and discontent. Technical students, moreover, tend to be more "professional" in their orientation than their liberal arts colleagues, and see their educational careers as preparation for specific occupations. This orientation tends to make them indifferent to political issues and less willing to risk their educational careers. In addition to the scientific, technical and liberal arts institutions, there are other institutions of higher education in Bombay affiliated to Bombay University. Many liberal arts colleges have commerce colleges affiliated to them. There are 4,632 commerce students in Bombay. The commerce course, which may be either undergraduate or post-graduate, prepares students for participation in commercial or business enterprises following graduation.

A number of specialized institutions exist in Bombay. The J. J. School of Art, which has a status as an institution of higher education, concentrates on both the creative and commercial aspects of art. The medical colleges, which have traditionally been an active segment of the student movement, constitute a substantial segment of the student community. There are four medical schools in Bombay with a combined enrollment of 2,420 students. Several of these colleges, with traditions dating from the early part of the Twentieth century, are among the best medical schools in India. Most concentrate on Western medicine, although there are institutions which offer courses in Ayurvedic (traditional) medicine.

The medical colleges offer the M.B.B.S. degree, which entitles the holder to practice as a general practitioner. Many medical students continue beyond this degree to specialize, while some go abroad for further medical education. Medical students are not subjected to the same type of frustration due to uncertain futures that most arts students are, for the demand for doctors is great and their incomes are comparatively high. Most medical students come from financially secure families; class differences among medical students are less than in the general student population. The medical curriculum is rigorous, consisting of a five year course, including both academic preparation and practical intern experience in a hospital.

Despite the fact that the medical colleges are of high quality and that the students do not suffer from the uncertainty which other students feel, the medical colleges have traditionally been active in the student movement. It has been postulated that a rigorous and well planned curriculum will prevent political involvement for the most part. This does not hold true, however, for the medical students, who have regularly gone on strike, both before and after Independence. Since Independence, the medical students have concentrated thir own campaigns on issues such as fee increases, curriculum, and living facilities. Medical students have also supported campaigns by doctors, hospital employees and others.

Medical students have been successful a rather substantial proportion of the time in their agitational campaign indicating the fact that they have been well organized and that their grievances have been well formulated. The various medical students' committees have generally presented limited demands to administrators and to the government, and through good publicity and efficient organization, have brought effective pressure on the authorities involved. The leadership of the medical students has usually been older, and probably more experienced than that of the general student movement.

One educational institution which has not been discussed in this section, but which is an important part of the educational complex in Bombay is S.N.D.T. University. Although this institution is not affiliated to the Bombay University, it has 4,640 students attending its affiliated colleges in Bombay and other areas of Maharashtra and Gujarat. The significant fact about this university is that it is limited to women and is one of the pioneering women's universities in India. In addition, it is the only institution of higher education in Bombay to offer instruction in both Marathi and Gujarati. S.N.D.T. University offers both bachelors and post-graduate degrees in various fields.

The curriculum at S.N.D.T. University does not differ substantially from the other colleges in the city, although it is probably somewhat less rigorous in its standards. Its admissions policies are more lax, and it does not claim to be a research institution, but rather a teaching institution for women students. The university is one of the newer institutions in Bombay, having been founded in 1916 and granted statutory recognition in 1951.

Student extra-curricular life at S.N.D.T. University and its affiliated colleges is active, although it has been under the strict supervision of the administration. Female students have not been traditionally active in the political life of the student community (with a few notable exceptions) and generally play a rather passive role in student affairs. It is not surprising, therefore, that extra-curricular activities at S.N.D.T. should be more restricted than at many other colleges in the city.

There are a number of teacher training institutions in the city. Probably the best known of these institutions is the St. Xavier's Institute of Education, offering only post-graduate training in various fields of education and related topics. Standards at this institution, as at most of the post-graduate institutions in the city, are high. The Institute is only a decade old and has 208 students, but it has succeeded in building up some impressive programs and traditions.

The student body of the Institute is conspicuously more heterogenous and is older than at most institutions. Many students are married, and a large number attend classes only part time, whil holding teaching positions at primary and secondary schools in the city. The Institute gets some state financial aid, enabling it to give scholarships to able students. No agitational issues have arisen during the ten years since the founding of the institution.

The variety and scope of the educational institution, in Bombay makes it difficult to generalize about the student population. The task of discussing "higher education" in Bombay is also more complex because of the plethora of institutions in the city and the differing pressures on each college or institute. It is hoped that by presenting a description of several fairly typical educational institutions, a clearer understanding of the context of student political and social activity can be gained.

PART II

The Context of Student Life: Bombay 1900-1965

CHAPTER III

THE ROOTS OF THE STUDENT MOVEMENT (1850-1935)

THERE IS a long tradition of serious-minded student extra-curricular activity in India. As early as 1848, Dadabhai Naoroji, the Parsi entrepreneur and reformer, founded a "Students' Scientific and Literary Society" to serve the small student population in Bombay. Typical of the efforts undertaken during this early period, this group served as a discussion center for several years. At many of Bombay's oldest educational institutions students showed an inclination toward debate and discussion during the years between 1850 and 1880. Student energies were also devoted to the expansion of college education for women, a radical innovation. During the 1880's, there was some agitation for holding the Indian Civil Service examinations in India instead of England, in order to eliminate the long journey for prospective Indian candidates. The Indian National Congress, then a moderate middle class organization without a specific political program, supported this reform measure; this was one of the first occasions when the student community and the Congress worked in cooperation.

Early Student Activity

By 1900, a number of student groups had developed, although educational matters and not politics were the main preoccupation. As one British observer has noted: "It was not till after political and racial excitement [of the nationalist movement] that the youth attending schools and colleges showed signs of turbulence and insubordination.[1] By 1905, students were awakening to the urgent relevance of political issues. Massive agitation in Bengal against the proposed British partition of the province succeeded, after some loss of life, in forcing the British to abandon this project. Sympathy demonstrations, spurred primarily by students, took place in

[1] Dinkia Sakrikar, "A History of the Student Movement in India" (typewritten manuscript, Bombay, 1946), p. 28.

other areas. This agitation, which was not coordinated by any all-India student organization, provided a "baptism of fire" for many Indian students, making them aware of their potential influence on politics. This awareness was particularly strong in Bengal, which had an independent political and literary tradition. The struggle against the partition lasted for seven years, though student activity was sporadic during the period. A few students, again mainly in Bengal, joined the nascent terrorist movement, and several were arrested for the attempted assassination of the Governor General while he visited one of the colleges in Calcutta. One observer has stated that a large proportion of the terrorist activity in Maharashtra as well as Bengal during this period was perpetrated by students. One of the key terrorist organizations at that time was the Hindustan Socialist Republican Army, which had strong student support.[2]

In Bombay, the Young India League was formed in 1906, primarily under the leadership of B. G. Tilak and the strongly traditionally minded nationalists of the day; it involved some of the Indian students who had received their college education in England. Although the League was short lived and unable to provide leadership to the student community in Bombay, it represented the first established student political organization in Bombay, providing the basis for future organizational efforts by training leaders and providing experience with parliamentary procedures.

1919 saw one of the first student strikes in the colleges of Bombay. One strike, which effectively closed the colleges for one day, was to protest the visit to Bombay of the Prince of Wales. Another agitation took place at Wilson College in Bombay, a missionary controlled institution, against the compulsory reading of Christian scriptures. Interestingly enough, one of the leaders of this agitation was S. A. Dange, later to become General Secretary of the Communist Party of India and an important Indian political figure. The agitation was also unsuccessful, although the principal agreed to discount the examination given on the Bible. These demonstrations took place without the benefit of any coordinating organization, and although there

---

[2] Interview with N. R. Phatak, Associate Director of the Maharashtra State Committee for a History of the Freedom Movement, March, 1965.

was, no doubt, communication among students at various colleges, no organization emerged from these agitational efforts.[3]

With minor exceptions, student agitation prior to 1920 was of a spontaneous and erratic nature and lacked any overall direction. It was primarily directed at local campus-oriented issues, and only a minor interest was taken in broader political issues. No real "movement" emerged during this period, although students began to realize that they could have a role in shaping their educational institutions. Attention was focused on local campus issues as well as broader political affairs, a fact that characterized the student movement in later periods as well. The fact that the movement lacked coordination and existed as an erratic series of isolated outbursts rather than an organized effort is also significant. Many observers claim that even at the zenith of its power—during the independence struggle—the movement lived from crisis to crisis, sustained only by the external events, and lacked form and continuity.

Gandhi's first mass movement, called in 1920 to apply pressure on the British for a favorable settlement of Muslim rights in Turkey, involved students on a national scale. The demands of the movement were soon enlarged to include nationalist slogans. The Non-Cooperation Movement sought to withdraw all Indian support from the British administered activities at every level. British goods were boycotted, and civil servants were asked to resign their posts in the British administration. Students were asked to leave British-run schools and colleges; many thousands of them heeded Gandhi's call.

In Bombay, the boycott of British schools was only partly successful, involving a minority of the students. Nevertheless, the boycott was a shock to the educational system and caused the creation of "national schools". These schools were founded by Congress activists to provide educational facilities for those students who had left their regular schools.

In October 1920, a series of public meetings were held to "seduce student from the schools and colleges attended by

[3] World Brotherhood, *A Survey of the Attitudes, Opinions, and Personality Traits of a Sample of Students at the University of Bombay*, (Bombay: World Brotherhood, 1960).

them".[4] Gandhi himself addressed Bombay college students on several occasions and sent a letter to the students of Wilson college. The students' first response was to ask college authorities to disassociate the colleges from the government. When this demand was refused, some left college. In 1921, the first national college was founded in Bombay with about 100 students; however, by 1924 it had shrunk to 65. The National Medical College, which has persisted to the present time, was started at that time, and by 1924, it had 450 students.[5] Pro-nationalist professors acted as teachers in these colleges, and despite very inadequate facilities, these unorthodox schools often provided excellent and dedicated instruction. Within a year after the founding of these colleges, most of the students who had left their regular institutions applied for readmission. With the exception of the National Medical College, all the national colleges ceased to exist.

In addition to heeding Gandhi's call for a boycott of the schools and colleges, the students were actively engaged in picketing shops selling British made goods and in promoting khadi (hand spinning) which was a primary aspect of Gandhi's program. One former student leader stated that the heroism of the students in the 1920's exceeded their activity in the 1942 movement, usually considered the zenith of the student struggle.[6]

1920 was also the year in which the first All-India College Students' Conference was held at Nagpur. The president of the meeting was the respected nationalist leader, Lala Lajpat Rai. At the meeting, a permanent organization, the Hind Vidyarthi Sabha (Indian Students' Organization), was formed, although it did not achieve notable success. It is interesting that a resolution for complete independence was tabled at this meeting; it failed by eleven votes despite the presence of many radical Congress leaders.[7] Its failure was probably due to the fact that the Congress itself was still debating the isue.

The Nagpur meeting was an important milestone in the deve-

[4] Government of Bombay, Commissioner of Police, "Report on National Schools and Colleges", 1920, p. 4.
[5] *Ibid.*, p. 6.
[6] Sakrikar, op. cit., p. 61.
[7] Ahluwalia, *op. cit.*, p. 2.

lopment of an Indian student movement. It is significant that the meeting took place in the midst of an important nationalist agitational campaign and was fostered mainly by adult nationalist leaders. Very few of the aims of the conference were translated into reality, since the enthusiasm generated by the meeting could not be sustained in the day to day functioning of the student organizations

Annual College Students' Conferences were held after 1920. These meetings attracted substantial participation from all parts of India. The second conference, held in Ahmedabad in 1920, was attended by 3,000 delegates. This meeting reaffirmed the loyalty of the students to the Congress; its resolutions echoed Gandhi's stress on constructive work, such as khadi and literacy campaigns. The strong nationalist and pro-Congress policy of the student movement was evident during this entire period.

Students in Bombay were also active in one of the first paramilitary organizations in India. The National Volunteer League was founded at the time of the Non-Cooperation Movement. Although the police considered it as a "disruptive and potentially dangerous element", the League functioned along Gandhian lines, keeping order at Congress meetings and engaging in constructive work.[8] Their distinctive uniforms and athletic drill were particularly disturbing to the government, which eventually banned the organization.

The next major agitational effort made by Bombay students took place in 1928, when the Simon Commission came to India to make proposals for Indian self-government. The Congress, which opposed the Commission because it did not include nationalist Indians, sought to arouse mass opposition to its visit. The students, who had lapsed into inactivity, again responded enthusiastically to the call and launched a number of demonstrations. For the first time, the student community took the responsibility for a series of demonstrations.

In Bombay, the students engaged in a one day strike from classes, passed resolutions against the Simon Commission at a mass meeting, and participated in a black flag demonstration and procession, during which several students were injured by

---

[8] Government of Bombay, Commissioner of Police, "Report on the National Volunteer Movement", 1935, p. 5.

the police. Since the Simon Commission disembarked at Bombay before beginning their survey, the actions of the Bombay students had repercussions in other parts of India, spurring on students in Lahore, Patna, and other cities. The Bombay demonstrations were organized by an ad hoc committee; however, the impetus came from members of the Students' Brotherhood. A number of the younger Bombay Congress leaders, such as S. K. Patil, who had recently graduated from the Students' Brotherhood, were active in organizing these demonstrations. The movement was able to organize itself on an on-going basis in Bombay and other cities and provide the organizational continuity necessary for sustained action. By providing the nucleus of leadership and an on-going organizational structure, the Brotherhood made it possible for student activists to take advantage of specific local situations since they could fall back on an existing group for support.

Subhas Chandra Bose, a pioneer youth leader and popular figure among the more radical Congress and socialist youth, correctly stated:

> The years 1928-29 witnessed an unprecedented awakening among the youths. The halting attitude of the Congress at Calcutta and the stale tactics of the Swarajists in legislatures aroused the youths to a sense of their duty.[9]

When Gandhi announced his civil disobedience campaign in 1930, the students in Bombay again responded to his call. The 1930 movement probably attracted a larger number of students than that of 1920, although only a minority of the student community took part in the agitation. By 1930, in Bombay a student organization, basically nationalist in its outlook and interested in political action, had been formed. The organization helped to coordinate student agitations, keeping in close contact with the Congress leaders. This group, the Bombay Youth League, was responsible for many of the mass student demonstrations, strikes, and other forms of protests which took place. Other student groups were created to deal with specific aspects of the nationalist cause. The Students' Anti-Untouchable Com-

---

[9] Sakrikar, *op. cit.*, p. 31.

mittee organized meetings and demonstrations against the concept of untouchability and sent students into the homes of untouchables to do social work. The Bombay Students' Swadeshi League carried on propaganda against the use of foreign made goods and held study circles on this topic.[10]

Students were involved in picketing of foreign shops, often constituting the spearhead of the Congress campaign. Whenever a student leader was arrested, demonstrations and protest meetings were called. Students at a the top ranking colleges, such as Wilson, St. Xavier's and Elphinstone, were enthusiastic supporters of this strike, whereas the strike was less effective at other colleges.[11] The students also organized what came to be known as the "army of monkeys", which consisted mainly of high school and college students. This "army" fought pitched battles with the police and distributed illegal Congress literature. Much of the terrorist activity which took place in Bombay was carried out by this small group, under the unofficial control of the Youth League.[12]

Prior to 1930, there was a steadily growing amount of student activity related to the nationalist struggle. Small groups of students interested in discussing serious topics formed study circles without much outside support or guidance. The Students' Brotherhood, to be discussed later in this chapter, was the largest of the student organizations at this time, although more limited groups also existed. During the late 1920's, a small group of college students, called the Rasputin Group, met regularly to discuss social, cultural and political issues. Each student prepared independent research on a specific topic for presentation before the group for discussion. Many of the active members of this group later entered politics.[13] In the early 1930's, the small Communist movement also made serious attempts to sponsor study circles; their efforts were well rewarded in the following decade, when many of the city's best students joined the ranks of the Communist student organization, the Bombay

[10] Prabadh Chandra, *Student Movement in India*, (Lahore: All-India Students' Federation, 1938), p. 37.
[11] *Bombay Chronicle*, July 2, 1930, p. 7.
[12] Sakrikar, *op. cit.*, p. 34.
[13] Interview with Soli Batliwala, former president of the Students' Brotherhood, November 30, 1964.

Students' Union, or their trade union or cultural fronts, such as the All-India Trade Union Congress or the Peoples' Theater. Groups such as the Young Men's Hindu Association, the Muslim Students' Union, and Parsi Students' Association, carried out active social and cultural programs with lecture series, important speakers and discussion. Although their activities were limited to the non-political, some students became introduced to other, more militant, student groups through these organizations.

The Students' Brotherhood (1920-1940)

One of the most important of Bombay's student organizations was the Students' Brotherhood. Founded in 1889, the Brotherhood was dedicated primarily to social and cultural activity, although it did help to sponsor some valuable social service work and in its latter period was much involved in political activities.

The origins of the Students' Brotherhood are unclear. There are records of the publication of the **Students' Brotherhood Quarterly** between 1907 and 1914. The journal featured articles of cultural and literary interest, with concentration on European rather than Indian topics. During this period, as well as throughout its history, the Brotherhood had the support of a number of prominent college principals, industrialists, and Christian missionaries. The journal stated its main purpose as being to "challenge the intellect of the students."[14]

During the 1920's and 1930's, the Students' Brotherhood constituted on eof the few available extra-curricular activities. The Brotherhood, because it served an important purpose in the student community and had adequate financial support and adult interest, maintained itself until the political struggles of the late 1930's distracted the attention of the student community, and the development of college-sponsored extra-curricular organizations supplanted it. The lack of a recognized extra-curriculum based in the colleges undoubtably made it easier for the unofficial student groups to obtain substantial support.

The leading activists in the Brotherhood were usually superior students at their respective colleges. Consequently, the Brother-

[14] *Students' Brotherhood Quarterly*, (Winter, 1917), p. 120.

hood resembled an interlooking directorate of student leaders in Bombay. Leading Brotherhood members also held positions in the Muslim, Parsi, and Hindu student organizations. Furthermore, the Brotherhood controlled a number of college unions, among which were those at Wilson, St. Xavier's, and Elphinstone Colleges.

The educational system was the subject of much discussion and debate at this time, and the Brotherhood arranged a number of lectures on administrative reform in the universities, the examination system, curriculum and similar topics. When the percentage of students passing the matriculation examination of 1927-28 fell steeply, the Brotherhood issued a protest and called the students into the streets. A march on the University of Bombay senate attracted more than 150 students; the demonstration later grew to 10,000 strong. The students stormed into the university convocation hall, where the senate was meeting, and forced a reconsideration of the results of the examination.

Despite this particular outburst of activism, the Brotherhood limited its activities for the most part to purely academic discussions of social issues. The Brotherhood (with premises where students could gather, talk and play games) was a meeting place for the student community. It was one of the few places where the students of different linguistic or religious groups could freely associate. The few women students at Bombay's colleges were also admitted into the organization, thereby making it one of the most socially advanced associations in Bombay. The integrating and modernizing function of the Brotherhood cannot be overemphasized. The discussions on political and social issues which took place at the headquarters of the Students' Brotherhood provided guidance for the student community, and coordinated actions were planned. Also of importance was the library of the Brotherhood, which was small but well selected.

The Students' Brotherhood sponsored an annual "intercommunal vegetarian dinner" with the Muslim Students' Union. This was one of the few opportunities at which Indians of different castes and communities could eat together; this in itself was a radical innovation for the time. Lectures were held once a week, including topics from English literature to the future of the nationalist movement in India. As time went on, the topics took on a political tone.

The Brotherhood served as a leadership training institute for many of its members. Students received training in public speaking, parliamentary procedures and methods of organizing meetings and projects; they learned all the organizational details which would become important during the nationalist struggle and afterwards in independent India. The list of the Brotherhood's prominent alumni is long. Several ministers of the Indian cabinet were members, as were many political leaders. Some alumni have gone to all extremes of the political spectrum; one former member is a leading figure in the left Communist Party; another is a leader of the conservative Swatantra Party.

Through its scholarship programs, the Brotherhood enabled a few students from lower middle class families to attend college at a time when the colleges were limited almost entirely to young upper class people. A sub-committee of the Brotherhood organized literacy campaigns in working class areas of Bombay. Students went to slums and taught hygiene. Preparatory classes for students facing their matriculation examinations were opened by the Brotherhood at the end of each school year. Some of this social service work was politically motivated, and Gandhi's call for constructive work having had a profound impact on the organization in the early 1930's.

After the Non-Cooperation Movement of 1920, the critical political situation in the country demand an increasingly greater involvement of the Brotherhood; as will be seen, this involvement eventually caused the collapse of the organization. After 1930, political groups recruited members through the Students' Brotherhood. Although a minority group, the Communist students were able, by virtue of concerted effort, were able to attract rank and file members of the Brotherhood with radical leanings. The Communists set up small study circles which met regularly to discuss such topics as the significance of the Russian revolution and the works of Marx and Lenin, and their implications for India. Though they had a later start, the Congress students workers did similar work in the Brotherhood and were able to build up support among Brotherhood members. As the general emphasis of the Brotherhood moved towards politics, the Congress and Communist factions within the organization occasionally clashed openly at meetings. By and large, however, their relations were amicable, and an attempt was made on both sides to avoid alienating the less politically-minded students by keeping purely political issues in the background.

The predominant political outlook among the students at this time was leftist. Even those students who followed Gandhi and were not attracted to the Communist faction were powerfully influenced by socialist and radical ideas. It is probable that students of that generation were more familiar with the work of Marx and Lenin than are the present Indian students. It was the British socialists, however, who had the most influence over the students. Men such as Sidney Webb, Harold Laski, and others were more potent ideological forces than either traditional Hindu scholarship or Marxism to the students of this generation.

By 1936, the atmosphere in India had become politicized due to the influence of Gandhi's mass movement, and the students were particularly taken up with political ideas and agitation, with many students taking a direct part in Congress affairs. The Students' Brotherhood, although it remained in existence until the beginning of the Second World War, became less important as the students moved toward more direct participation in politics.

The Youth League — Politics and the Student Movement

Organizations, particularly those formed to meet a particular crisis or situation, are indicative of the society from which they spring. The formation of the Bombay Youth League and similar organizations in other parts of India reflected a definite metamorphosis in the student movement. The growth of the Youth League was a recognition that politics had become a major concern of the student community. The Youth League was founded in 1927 to provide nationalist students with a forum for their activities. It was openly political from the beginning and often played an important role in the nationalist movement.

The membership of the Youth League and the Students' Brotherhood overlapped, although the Brotherhood, because of its history and diverse program, had a much wider base of membership. Despite its name, the Youth League consisted almost entirely of students, although occasional attempts were made to recruit non-students.

One of the key figures in the organization of the Youth League was Yusuf Meherally, a leading Bombay nationalist, pioneer socialist, and Muslim. This remarkable figure, whose career spanned the major part of the nationalist struggle in Bombay, was a mentor and guide to politically minded students. He opened his library, one of the most extensive in Bombay, to the students, giving many of them their first introduction to Marx, Laski, the Webbs, and other radical thinkers.[15]

The League arranged meetings from time to time to hear nationalist leaders. The most popular leaders among the students, Nehru, Subhas Chandra Bose, and Meherally himself, were leftists. The League provided a forums for left wing Congressman to speak. Study circles were organized on political topics, occasionally coordinated with activities of the Students' Brotherhood. The League organized excursions from Bombay for purposes of social service work and nationalist propaganda in the surrounding villages. These trips gave the predominantly middle and upper class students from Bombay a rare opportunity to see something of rural India.

When Gandhi was actively involved in helping the peasants of the Bardoli district of Gujarat in their struggle against oppressive land rents, the Youth League in Bombay took up their cause; food and funds were collected for the peasants, and the students sent a delegation to Bardoli to deliver the aid and to investigate the situation first hand.[16] In 1928, an evening school was set up by the students in a working class area of Bombay, and free literacy classes were taught by college students. For almost five years, an active program of lectures, social service work, discussions, and occasionally direct action projects, were undertaken by the Bombay Youth League.

A Bombay police report gives an indication of the scope of

[15] Interview with S. Natarajan, journalist, February 27, 1965.
[16] *Bombay Chronicle*, October 5, 1928, p. 4.

the League's activities:

The Bombay Youth League has recently published an account of its activities up to 1930, and boasts that its workers have been at the helm of all the fighting activities of the Congress during the civil disobedience movement, and that it supplies a large proportion of the "dictators" of the "war councils".[17]

The students were very active in the 1930 civil disobedience movement and were fond of such titles as "commander of the militia", "war councils", and "dictator", even though virtually all of their activity was non-violent and their organizational functioning democratic. During the 1930 movement, the Youth League virtually disappeared as an independent entity and merged with the local Congres leadership, providing the adult organization with many of its most active cadres. In 1932, when the Congress and the government came to terms, the students were somewhat unwilling to call off the struggle.

After the 1930 movement was brought to an end by Gandhi, the activity of the Youth League decreased, although it continued to exist with an active program for a number of years. The League turned its attention to local college affairs for the most part, although it continued to be interested in political matters. The Youth League was also given credit for frustrating two government attempts to increase college and school fees in 1930 and 1931.[18]

One of the most important aspects of the Youth League's activity is that it served as a model for other similar organizations in other parts of India. Students in colleges from Madras to Calcutta became involved in politics for the first time during this perod. Youth League organizers visited other university centers and tried to stimulate political activity. The annual meetings of Indian students assumed new vigor, and Bombay students took a leading role at these all-India conferences. These meetings were generally held at the some time and place as the annual sessions of the Indian National Congress and were

---

[17] Government of Bombay, Commissioner of Police, "General Survey of Civil Disobedience Movement in Bombay to 191", p. 30.

[18] Bombay Chronicle, February 28, 1931, p. 6.

often adjuncts of the Congress movement. While the early all-India student meetings lacked a well defined program and were as much social and cultural as political, the sessions after 1930 were clearly political, and took a radical stance on most issues.

Between 1928 and 1936, the Youth League in Bombay was able to function effectively as a political organization involving substantial numbers of students. Its meetings were generally well attended, and its small study circles were probably the most effective means then in existence of political education among students. The Youth League was among the most militant organizations in Bombay, often spearheading Congress activities and continually pressing the adult Congress organization for a more radical position. The League's activities were open to students from all of the city's colleges. Study groups met once or twice a week and attracted groups of between fifteen and seventy-five students regularly. In addition to the literacy classes, League members again ran sewing classes for women in the slums, did construction work in untouchable areas, and taught hygiene to both children and adults. Of particular significance is the fact that a fairly large number of women were members.

The League represented an important turning point for the student movement in Bombay. As the first specifically political student organization, the League introduced the student population to the intricacies of ideological politics. It gave a substantial number of students training in public speaking, organizational work, and in practical politics.

Conclusions

This early period in the development of the student movement in Bombay is, in some ways, one of its most important, for it set the pattern for student activity until 1947. It was a time of awakening political and social concern among students. The student organizations formed during this period had a profound impact on succeeding organizations, and the political ideologies pioneered by student leaders during the early 1930's remained strong during following periods.

The causes for the growth of student organizations, which was

unprecedented in Indian history, seem to be rooted mainly in
the growth of an educated and increasingly politicized urban
middle class and a substantial development of an independent
urban intelligentsia composed of lawyers, doctors, middle-
level government officials, and a few writers and journalists.
The diffusion of European education and Western political ideas,
as well as a world-wide revolutionary ferment and the rise of
nationalism in the colonial areas of the world in the past half
century, also stimulated the growth of student political
awareness.[19]

The development of a student movement must be seen in
the context of political events in India. The upsurge of nationalism, indicated first by the cultural reformers of Bengal and
other parts of India, and later in the terrorist movements, again
centered in Bengal, stimulated the middle-class Indian National
Congress to gradually take a more militant position, and eventually, under Gandhi's leadership, to lead the nationalist struggle.

The organizational pattern of the student movement during
this period of growth of student groups in Bombay reflects
broader trends in Indian politics. The transformation from the
moderate Students' Brotherhood to the more militant and more
specifically political Youth League happened on a more massive
scale in the broader political movements. The shifting popularity of the student movement on the college campuses also
reflects the broader social movements of the times, which were
unable to sustain themselves during periods of inactivity for
the most part. There does not seem to be a clear-cut pattern
of organizational succession, except for the forces that have
been mentioned which manifested themselves from the outside
environment. The leadership of the movement remained in
the hands of upper class politically oriented students, who began
to experiment with agitational politics and with ideological
issues during this period.

Although higher education in Bombay showed some signs of
change during this period, the student population remained
fairly compact and homogeneous. Its size and the number of

[19] For a more complete discussion of the impact of Western ideas,
particularly in education, on the Indian nationalist movement, see McCully,
op. cit.

colleges rose slowly during the early 1930's, with the great expansion coming in later years. Bombay's few colleges were in fairly close communication, and there was something of a sense of community among the students. India's political climate was changing during this period, and the student organizations showed something of this shift in attitudes. Western political ideologies, from Marxism to liberalism, had a strong impact on politically minded students. The student political groups that were formed reflected Western ideological and organizational trends.

While extra-curricular activities did exist prior to 1920, a dramatic growth in such activities took place between 1920 and 1935. Primarily through student initiative, organizations of various kinds were formed. Educational administrators were relatively liberal in their controls for student groups, and literary and cultural groups of various kinds flourished. Groups like the Students' Brotherhood were a transition between the militant political groups of the nationalist period and the cultural concerns of earlier periods, for the Brotherhood combined political discussion and debate with social service activity. Constructive social work served as a means of political experience without arousing government opposition.

CHAPTER IV

THE POLITICIZATION OF THE STUDENT MOVEMENT
1935-1942

DURING THE Thirties, the nationalist movement came of age. In modern terminology, it became a ' 'national liberation movement", one of the first such movements which took on the accoutrements of a modern ideology, well developed organizational tactics, and a charismatic leader. However, the Congress also drew from the deep well of Indian tradition; its leader, Mahatma Gandhi, constituted a fitting, if sometimes frustrating, combination of the modern and the traditional.

The decade culminating with the "Quit India" struggle of 1942 brought large sections of the Indian population, previously uninvolved in political affairs, into a militant struggle. For the urban masses in particular, the independence struggle was a political baptism. The students, although involved in politics to some extent prior to 1930, assumed positions of initiative and responsibility for the struggle in the 1930's and 1940's. By 1942 they were ready to assume some of the leadership of the Congress when the adult leaders were jailed and the party had been banned by the British after August 9, 1942.

The transformation of the Congress into a broad based mass movement moved the thinking of the student organizations unmistakably beyond local campus issues and into national politics. Even campus-oriented agitations were more frequently linked to an outside political issue. Student strikes were usually in retaliation to a regulation imposed by the British. The student organizations worked in close collaboration with outside groups, becoming in many ways adjuncts of the national political organizations. The Congress, the Congress Socialists and the Communists each sought to guide the student movement toward a program most advantageous to its own policies; naturally, the political groups used the movement as a recruiting ground.

As a growing minority of the students became involved in he nationalist struggle, it was inevitable that politics would enter the college campuses. India's educational institutions, which had previously maintained neutrality on most political issues while retaining a basic loyalty to the British Raj, were forced into the struggle by the militant student movement. The injection of politics into the educational system and the increased contact between the college and the broader society has continued to have important implications to the present time. Bombay, being one of the main centers of the struggle, was more deeply involved in the agitational movement than most other urban centers in India.

Political Student Activity

The organizational framework of the Bombay student movement is rather complicated and, because of its fluidity, difficult to comprehend. While the specific organizational forms which the movement took during this period are not so important, it is necessary to obtain some understanding of them in order to perceive the rapidly changing political situation. In the mid 1930's, another set of organizations emerged. The Bombay Presidency (Provincial) Students' Federation was created after a well attended student conference in Bombay in 1936. The Federation served the students in the whole of Bombay Presidency, although its nucleus was in the city of Bombay. The local affiliate o the Federation was the Bombay Students' Union, also founded around 1936. Since the organizational bases of both groups were in Bombay city and its suburbs, and their political programs were almost identical, it was often difficult to differentiate these groups in a given situation. Leadership of the groups was interrchangeable.

On the lowest level, the Bombay Students' Union was divided into three units, the North Bombay Students' Union, the Bombay Suburban Students' Union, and the Bombay Students' Union (South). The Students' Federation had representatives from these three groups on its working committee, as well as representation from student organizations in other areas of the Presidency. The B.P.S.F. was, in turn, affiliated to the All-India Students' Federation, the nationalist student organization functioning for the whole subcontinent. The A.I.S.F. met each year, usually at the site of the annual session of the Congress and brought student leaders from all parts of India together, giving them a chance to meet such national leaders as Nehru and Subhas Chandra Bose. Bombay students took an active part in the functioning of the A.I.S.F.

Other organizational structures also existed in Bombay. Groups such as the National Youth League, the Progressive Group and other organizations existed for short periods of time, or during a specific agitational campaign. Usually "front" groups of the nationalist movement, these groups have little significance as independent entities and will therefore not be dealt with in detail.

The most important of the nationalist student organizations was the Bombay Students' Union. All factions worked within this organization, often leading to heated debates on matters of policy, and the organizations gave the leadership to the students in the various agitations of the Thirties. By the end of the decade, the Communist and non-Communist leftist elements within the movement could no longer co-exist, and the B.S.U. formally split into two organizations in 1940.

Bombay's first student conference was held in June 1930; at this meeting student leaders were able to agree on a common program to help the Congress. As the *Bombay Chronicle* stated in an editorial:

> The Bombay Student Conference showed the political temper of India's younger generation — a warning to the British and to India's nationalist leaders to hold fast.[1]

The newly formed nationalist student movement had the blessings and active support of the Congress. Some of the best students in Bombay were involved in the organization from the beginning; the association of superior students with the movement continued until 1947, thereby providing the student movement with intelligent leadership.

To coordinate its work, the B.S.U. elected a working committee, which consisted of representatives from each of the colleges and from selected secondary schools. This body met

[1] *Bombay Chronicle*, July 1, 1930, p. 6.

as often as necessary to decide policy and to run the organization. In its attempt to organize cells in each of the colleges, the B.S.U. was moderately successful. Several chapters of secondary school students were also organized. Activities sponsored by the Bombay Students' Union included a student sponsored *Swadeshi* (Indian made articles) exhibition. Many students left their colleges for the villages to work on construction and literacy projects. When the Congress was banned by the British authorities, students were primarily responsible for the production and distribution of the clandestine *Congress Bulletin* and other propaganda work.

The functioning of the organization was basically democratic. When the ideological lines within the student movement became clearly drawn in the mid-Thirties, the B.S.U. was always sure to include a sufficient number of Gandhian, socialist and Communist students on the Working Committee to assure harmony. Decisions were reached by the committee on the basis of an agreement between these groups.

The Bombay Students' Union entered the broader political movements of the city. Students became active in labor organizing and worked with the Communists and, after 1934, with the Congress Socialists. The students were a valuable source of active cadres to the trade union movement. Students were a radical element in the Congress. Moreover, the student movement publicly demanded complete independence before the Congress had officially adopted this policy in January of 1930. Gandhi himself felt constrained to write to the Bombay Students' Union, asking them to moderate their views and to follow the leadership of the Congress.[3] The students actively worked against communalism, and called on both the Congress and the broader community to resist communalist tendencies. When Congress leaders were on the verge of accepting the British scheme of separate electorates for Hindus and Muslims, the Union spoke out strongly against this plan, charging that it would foster communalism. When the R.S.S., a right-wing Hindu communalist organization began to attract a substantial amount of young people to its para-military exercises, the

[2] *Bombay Chronicle*, July 22, 1930, p. 3.
[3] *Bombay Chronicle*, June 7, 1931, p. 5.

Students' Federation took action. Similarly, there was some concern that the Congress was losing ground to the Hindu Mahasabha on the one hand and the Muslim League on the other. The Federation organized a large youth railly and conference. The conference was very successful, with more than 2,000 delegates from Bombay state attending. The conference received massive publicity and proved a serious setback for the R.S.S. and the other communalist groups.

The B.S.U. continued to organize a number of agitations at various colleges. Taking advantage of local grievances, the B.S.U. fostered the maximum amount of disturbance. One of these strikes took place at Wilson College, in 1932, and for two days the entire student body stayed on strike in protest against the expulsion of a student for his pro-Congress activities.[4] The aim of these agitations was to embarrass the British authorities. The government responded by declaring a number of student and youth organizations in Bombay illegal. Despite this serious harassment and the arrest of several student leaders, the student movement continued to function.

The following will give an indication of the activity of the student movement in the campaigns of the early 1930's:

In the 30's, street corner meetings were held to rouse public opinion. Small detachments of 25 Youth Guards used to march carrying national flags, bugles, and posters. At every street corner, this small procession would stop and Meherally would get on top of a car and deliver fiery speeches urging people to boy-cott British goods. Thousands of leaflets were distributed and hundreds of meetings were held.[5]

Later, when the Congress formed its first "War Councils", four of its members were from the student movement, and Meherally, who was president of the Youth League at that time, became Commander of the Congress Volunteers, many of whom were recruited from the student movement.

By 1935, the Bombay Students' Union was a recognized

[4] *Bombay Chronicle*, August 29, 1932, p. 8.
[5] P. M. Joshi, "Inspiring Saga of India's Rebel Youth Movement", *Blitz*, August 4, 1946, p. 46.

organization with something of a tradition. It was able to maintain a membership of about 5,000 until the organization split in 1940.[6] Most of the members of the B.S.U. were from the middle class, although many of the leaders were wealthier students. There were fewer girls than men in the organization, although considering the Indian social structure the number of women was surprisingly large.[7] Most of the membership was Hindu, although there were a few Parsis and Christians. Muslims were conspicuous by their absence. There were probably more Gujaratis than Maharashtrians in the organization, possibly because of Gandhi's influence in the Bombay area at this time. The Students' Union was one of the few organizations in Bombay which had a cosmopolitan membership able to work closely together.

Many Muslim students, formerly part of the nationalist student movement, quit at the urging of the newly formed Muslim League, forming the All-India Muslim Students' Federation. Other minority groups formed separate organizations at this time, such as the Scheduled Caste (Untouchables) Students' Federation, the Sikh Students' Federation. These groups were, however, small and weak by comparison. As the decade drew to a close, even the predominantly Hindu nationalist student movement split on ideological lines, thus making the bifurcation of the student movement almost complete.[8]

The Round Table Conferences, and other political maneuverings of the Congress leadership and the British during the late Thirties drew little response from the student movement, although the active student workers naturally watched these events with great interest. The student movement, forced to depend upon its own resources during this period, turned to the familiar social service and educational tasks: well organized literacy programs were planned for the villages surrounding Bombay, and several hundred students regularly spent their vacations doing village work. Nationalist propaganda

[6] Interview with M. L. Shah, former General Secretary of the All India Students' Federation, November 29, 1964.

[7] Interview with Usha Mehta, Department of Politics, University of Bombay, January 11, 1965.

[8] Ahluwalia, *op. cit.*

was an important part of these literacy campaigns. Medical students were active in introducing public health measures to the villages. Cultural groups were sent to teach national songs and perform plays.[9] Students were very much involved with the Congress Volunteer Corps, which engaged in social service work in addition to acting as guards at political meetings. One of the most original ideas that was developed by the Students' Union and the Bombay Presidency Students' Federation was sending small groups of students to villages to stay in one place for a period of time. The students were also teaching Hindustani, reaching some 10,000 people in Bombay over a two year period.

Under the sporsorship of the Students' Brotherhood, the Students' Union and other organizations in Bombay, an all-city students meeting was convened in June of 1936. Stimulated in part by the militant student response to the matriculation massacre demonstration and public indignation engendered in favour of the students, the purpose of the meeting was to investigate student grievances and communicate the opinions of the students to the administrative authorities in a disciplined yet forceful manner. The meeting was organized by nationalist students with strong backing from the leftists. The meeting drew more than a thousand students. The Students' Character which has drawn up became a pioneering statement which was influential on students in other parts of India.

The conference passed a resolution stating for the first time that students had an inherent right to organize to present their grievances. The resolution read as follows:

This meeting recognizes the inherent rights, as citizens, of the students to organize themselves with a view to represent their grievances and protest against any injustice or ill treatment meted out to them. This meeting emphatically condemns the presence of the police in the Senate Hall on Monday last, and the handing over the University Gardens to the armed police by the university authorities on Tuesday, thereby conveying a threat of violent repression of the students in their

---

[9] Interview with G. S. Pohekar, former editor of the *Students' Call*, March 15, 1965.

legitimate demonstration of discontent against the disgraceful treatment meted out to them...............[10]

More important than this resolution, however, was the Charter itself. The Charter spelled out some of the specific issues of vital importance to the student community. It stated in part:

> Freedom of thought, speech and association.......are considered and granted as indispensable essentials of civilized life.

> The State shall recognize organizations of students in the same way and to the same extent as it recognizes organizations of workers, consumers, or merchants, and shall in all matters affecting education and well being of the student community, ordinarily act through such organizations, with the view to developing habits of self-government, discipline, and teamwork among the students.[11]

These few quotations from the Charter will give an indication of its style and comprehensive contents.

With the adoption of the Charter, the student organizations in Bombay took more interest in educational issues. In 1937, for instance, the Bombay Presidency Students' Federation submitted a memorandum to the Minister of Education demanding a democratization of education and asking that the post of Vice Chancellor be elective rather than nominative. The students also asked that legislation be passed freeing the secondary schools from government control. On another occasion, the students protested against an official refusal to hold the matriculation examination twice in one year. The student movement was free to devote more attention to educational issues during this period because of the absence of an intense political struggle.

The Bombay Presidency Students' Conference of 1937 was a typical meeting. The meeting adopted the Charter of Rights, as well as expressly condemning the university for the 1936 matriculation massacre. A resolution supporting the Congress

[10] *Bombay Chronicle*, June 22, 1936, p. 16.
[11] *Ibid.*, p. 12.

swadeshi campaign was hotly debated and finally passed by a small majority.[12]

The 1938 meeting of the Bombay Students' Conference indicated some of the ideological trends taking place in the student movement. Called at the initiative of the Bombay Students' Union, which was strongly under the control of nationalist and anti-Communist elements, the conference was repeatedly disrupted by some of the Communist delegates from the North Bombay Students' Union. While both groups were still functioning in the same organization at this time, there was a good deal of infighting taking place. More than 500 delegates attended the conference and audiences of more than 2,000 attended many of the sessions. Despite a number of disruptions, the conference passed resolutions calling for an anti-imperialist struggle against Fascism and criticising some of the more conservative Congressmen for their compromising attitude toward the British. Many of the newspapers reacted negatively to the proceedings in 1938. For the first time, the simmering dispute between the Communists and non-Communists came into the open.

After 1937, the student movement in Bombay concentrated on political issues. Sympathy demonstrations and meetings were held to express solidarity with students in other parts of India when repressive actions were taken. In Bombay, the B.S.U. successfully defended several high school students arrested in a demonstration and secured their release from prison. The journal of the B.S.U. concentrated on political and agitational issues, although it served as a medium of communication for Bombay students as well. There is also no doubt that the movement spent increasingly more time on the factional disputes which began to come into the open in 1936 and 1937.

One of the major demonstrations of this latter period was against the visit of Sir Maurice Dwyer to Bombay. Dwyer was the Vice Chancellor of Delhi University who had expelled some of the nationalist students there. The Bombay Students' Union organized massive demonstrations wherever Dwyer spoke in Bombay and involved thousands of students. Some

---

[12] *Bombay Chronicle*, January 4, 1937, p. 7.

fifty students were arrested for blocking passage during one of these demonstrations.[13]

There is no doubt that the nationalist student groups were an important force on the campus. The Bombay Students' Union built up a highly committed and politically sophisticated group of activists during the 1930's, and had a profound influence on this group of individuals, which numbered in the hundreds. The fact that a number of prominent Bombay political leaders, trade union workers, intellectuals, and businessmen emerged from this relatively small group is highly significant. With 5,000 members, the nationalist student organizations also influenced larger numbers of students.

As has been noted, the student movement devoted itself almost exclusively to political issues, and only considered educational problems when they concerned the nationalist cause. As a result, the student movement had almost no influence on university reform or on broader issues of educational policy, other than to apply pressure in specific instances of administrative misconduct. The nationalist students may have had some impact on national policies through their active role in Gandhi's campaigns, and it is fairly clear that the Bombay Students' Union was a radicalizing influence on the Congress movement in the city, and it served as an organizational base for many of the Congress Socialist leaders.

The Socialist Student Front

The Congress Socialist Party, which was founded in 1934, had a strong influence on the student movement. Some of its leaders were popular student leaders recently graduated from the movement. Subhas Chandra Bose, M. R. Masani, Yusuf Meherally, Ashoka Mehta, Ram Manohar Lohia and many others were leading C.S.P. figures and popular among the students. The socialist leaders combined a number of advantages in dealing with the students. They were generally younger than the other Congress leaders. They were not committed to the Gandhian principle of non-violence. On the contrary, the socialist leaders pressed for more radical mass action, actively

[13] Interview with Pravina Mehta, former Poona student activist, March 11, 1965.

calling for a mass movement against the British. Their ideological position was radical: British imperialism was to be crushed by a revolutionary upsurge of the Indian masses. Furthermore, Indian capitalists and landowners were to be removed so that a democratic social system could be established. The keynote was action, and stress was placed on the industrial workers in the urban areas and on the students. Although the socialists gained some following among the peasant movements, thir main strength was in the cities and larger towns.

The Communist Student Front

The Communists were intent on maximizing their influence among the students, enabling them to enlist the student movement for any of the political campaigns which they might sponsor.[14] They were also interested in spreading Maxism among the students so as to increase the vanguard for a possible revolutionary movement in India.

The basis of the early influence of Communism in the student community in Bombay was the informal study circles which were organized. Under the leadership of men like S. A. Dange, who was himself involved in the student movement, and M. N. Roy, then a prominant Communist leader who spoke occasionally to Bombay students, a number of study circles were organized. Marxist theory proved an important part of the discussions, and the students read Marx, Lenin, and Stalin.[25] Serious discussions of the Russian revolution and its impact on India were also held. Radical literature clandestinely imported from England and occasionally from the Soviet Union was passed from student to student. These study circles, although guided by Communists, were relatively free and open; occasionally such "heretical" writers as Trotsky and Max Eastman were discussed by the group.

The Communist students were particularly successful at Elphistone College. They were able to build up their influence slowly but effectively, finally gaining control over many of the

---

[14] Interview with Batliwala, *loc. cit.*

[15] Interview with Krishnakant Desai, Advocate, Bombay High Court, March 2, 1965.

student organizations in the college. Beginning in 1939, the Communists set up small discussion groups for students which met regularly each week. The attendance at these groups ranged from ten to twenty, and many of the most able students in the college were involved, since the opportunity for serious discussion was otherwise rather limited. Such topics as the Russian revolution, the Indian national movement and matters of economics and politics were discussed in some depth. Most of these galterings were held in he student hostels, and were in no sense closed meetings.

In addition to these study groups for advanced students, efforts were made to attract students who were sympathetic to leftist ideas. The Communists were able to retain 60 per cent of their active members as active cadres.[16] Trained leaders taught student cadres the intricacies of organizing meetings, of public speaking, and other indispensable details.[17]

Until the split in the student movement in 1940, the Communist students generally worked within the other student organizations. In most cases, they supported the leadership of the Congress Socialists; their slogan was a "national front" against imperialism and reaction. The Communists consistently supported the Socialists against the Gandhians, assuring a leftist majority. They were occasionally able to assume a dominating position in some groups; the North Bombay Students' Union, for instance, remained in their control until the 1942 movement caused a shift in the leadership. They were of the opinion that although Gandhi himself was a good man he had been unduly influenced by wealthy groups within Indian society. Communist student leaders were models of progressive ideas and modernization to their student peers. Communist students were free from communal projudice and advocated female equality.

When the Second World War broke out in 1939, Communist students were active in the struggle against Indian participation. The Communist International opposed this "war between imperialists". Under the slogan of "not a man, not a rupee for war", the students engaged in an active propaganda cam-

---

[16] Interview with Batliwala, *loc. cit.*
[17] Interview with A. N. Namjoshi, December 29, 1964.

paign against the war; many Communist student leaders were arrested during 1939 and 1940 because of their participation in the agitation. The nationalist and socialist students were also involved in the anti-war struggle, but were not as militant at this time as were the Communists. The arrest of many key Communist student leaders caused serious dislocation in the student movement, and the Communists were hard pressed to maintain their hold. The arrested leaders served up to two years in jail; they were released only when the Communist Party line was again revised to support the war after the Soviet Union became involved in the European conflict.

The All India Students Federation and The Split in the Student Movement (1940)

The All-India Students' Federation, founded in 1936 with the support of the Congress, was conceived as the student wing of the Indian nationalist movement. No detailed ideological policy was marked out for the organization. Only frankly communalist elements were not welcomed into the organization. In the A.I.S.F., Gandhians, socialists, Communists, and independent radicals worked in cooperation. The first conference of the A.I.S.F., held in Lucknow in 1936, was addressed by both Nehru and M. A. Jinnah. Subhas Chandra Bose attended the meeting and served as president of the organization for several years. The first meeting was attended by 986 delegates. A series of resolutions were passed, most of which were prompted by the political situation in India. A resolution defining the role of students in politics was the topic of a heated debate. The matter was finally submitted to Nehru for solution, and he suggested a draft resolution which urged the students to take part in the national movement.[18]

During 1937 and 1938, the A.I.S.F., from its central offices in Bombay, sought to coordinate the activities of its affiliated groups, one of the strongest of which was the Bombay Presidency Students' Federation. In August of 1937, the A.I.S.F. working committee issued a call for students throughout India

[18] Sakrikar, *op. cit.*, p. 54.

to agitate for a number of demands. Among these proposals were:

1. 50 per cent reduction in college and examination fees.
2. Objectivity in textbooks with regard to Indian nationalism.
3. Freedom of speech in and out of schools.
4. The compulsory learning of the vernacular and Hindustani.
5. Compulsory recognition of student unions by university administrations.
6. Prohibition of communal student organizations.
7. Abolition of "degrading punishment".[19]

These demands were based more on a desire to create an atmosphere for agitational politics within the colleges than to seriously attempt to reform aspects of the university educational system.

At its annual session, held in Madras in January 1938, the first open split between the communists and the socialists occurred. M. R. Masani, then a prominent socialist leader, has stated that many of the socialist leaders were trying to create a split in the organization, and that the Communist students conveniently swallowed the bait.[20] When the Communist delegates proposed a resolution praising the newly implemented Soviet constitution, the socialists claimed that this subject had no place in the context of the Indian student movement. The Communist students succeeded in having the resolution approved by the Subjects Committee of the conference, but when they moved it onto the floor of the session, they met with determined socialist opposition.[21]

When the session reconvened the next day, the Communists called their own meeting and passed the resolution in question. The socialists and Gandhians also met separately, under Masani's leadership. Both groups claimed to be the "legitimate" All-India Students' Federation, and a good deal of confusion

[19] Reddy, op. cit., p. 140.
[20] Interview with M. R. Masani, Chairman of the Swatantra Party, December 29, 1964.
[21] Sakrikar, op. cit., p. 58.

was created as the delegates departed for home. A majority
of the delegates probably sided with the non-Communist forces
at this time, although the Communists were well organized. It
is probably true that the non-Communists had prevented a
determined Communist bid to take over the student movement
at the Madras session, since there is every indication that the
latter had planned their tactics well in advance.[22]

The two groups left Madras determined to press their claims
to legitimacy. After several months of functioning as separate
entities, both groups submitted to talks with several prominent
leftist Congress leaders and were persuaded to heal their split.
The national leaders, who had been quite concerned about the
student movement, expressed their satisfaction with the healing
of the split. Nehru stated on the occasion:

> All good wishes to the Students' Federation. I am glad
> that they have ended their petty arguments about trivial in-
> cidents. If they are to be worth anything they have to keep
> above such minor conflicts and think of the larger issues.
> To that end they should address themselves.[23]

The Nagpur session of the All-India Students' Federation,
held in December of 1940, saw the final split in the Indian
student movement. The 400 delegates who attened (representing nearly 40,000 members) were prepared for political debate,
since the situation in India had grown tense, and the student
movement was in a state of flux. Some of the Congress and
Communist underground leadership, who were in hiding at the
time, actually attended the sessions and gave advice to the
student leaders.[24] Conflicts in the executive committee had
paved the way for more disputes at the conference itself. A
number of observers have pointed out that the real reason for
the split was the growing animosity between the socialists and
the Communists, and that the apparent causes were merely
camouflage for this dispute.[25]

[22] Reddy, *op. cit.*, p. 145.
[23] *Bombay Chronicle*, February 26, 1938, p. 13.
[24] Interview with Desai, *loc. cit.*
[25] Gene Overstreet and Marshall Windmiller, *Communism in India* (Bombay: Perennial Press, 1960), p. 397.

Two separate sessions of the All-India Students' Federation were held, each passing resolutions, electing officers, and charting programs for the year. Each group stated its commitment to student unity and blamed the other for causing the split in the first place. The Communist students took the opportunity to launch a bitter attack on Gandhian non-violence, stating that India was ripe for a revolutionary struggle.[25] The socialist students, who were joined by the Gandhians and other independent groups, reiterated their faith in the Congress leadership and pledged to struggle for Indian independence. They attacked the Communists as tools of the Kremlin. When the groups left Nagpur, the lines of conflict were so firmly drawn that later attempts to reach a settlement of the problem were doomed to failure.

The Communists continued to use the name of the All-India Students' Federation, while the socialist-Gandhian group eventually changed their name to the All-India Students' Congress to avoid further confusion. In Bombay, the confusion was multiplied, since there were also two Bombay Students' Unions. The Nagpur split had important consequences for the entire student movement in India. Smaller splits took place in almost every local student group, ending the era of combined agitational effort. After 1940, the warring factions of the student movement spent almost as much time fighting each other as they did in working against the British. Surprisingly enough, the split which took place in the student movement did not seriously hamper its activity.

In Bombay, the student movement continued much as before, but with an increased militancy, for the Congress was beginning to wage an even more determined battle for complete independence. The Communists continued to function although the almost complete shift in the Party line when the Soviet Union entered the war threw the Indian Communists into confusion. It was months before the Communist organizations in India shifted from their militant anti-war position to support of the "Peoples' War" and the fight against fascism. Almost overnight, the Communists changed from a vocal opposition to the British to active supporters of British foreign policy. Many of the Communist student leaders were bewildered by this change of position, and a large number did not accept the explanation of the shift that was given by the Party leadership. As a result, the Communist student organizations, as well as other Communist front groups in India, lost large segments of their followers. The nationalist organizations, on the other hand, grew tremendously owing to the influx of former Communists and others who joined the movement in the heat of the struggle.

The student movement in Bombay was active in the national struggle. Each of the factions of the student movement actively supported the efforts of its parent group. The Communist students sent workers to help the All-India Trade Union Congress organize workers in the Bombay textile mills. Students constituted an important segment of the Communist volunteers corps and were active in Communist front cultural groups and in other activities. Similarly, the nationalists generally moved off the campus and into the streets. The students were not particularly enthusiastic about Gandhi's call for individual **satayagraha**, and preferred mass agitation instead. Nevertheless, they helped the Congress organization in its work, and probably constituted a majority of the Congress volunteers who acted as guards at political meetings and did social service work.

On the campuses, the student movement was interested mainly in embarrassing the authorities and the British administration. Strikes, when they occurred, were usually not aimed at improving campus conditions or pressing for educational reforms, but were purely political in nature. The period directly prior to 1942 can be seen as a preparation for the most important struggle in which the Indian nationalist movement was to engage. Organizationally and politically, this period prepared the student organizations, of all political views, for this struggle.

Educational Developments and Student Activity

Despite the importance of the political movements taking place in Bombay and in the rest of India, most students continued to be oriented towards the campus. In the excitement of the movement it is easy to overlook the fact that only a minority of students took a consistent interest in national and local politics. The period of the Thirties was an important one for Bombay's colleges, as it saw major expansion in college enrollments. A number of new colleges were established, and educational institutions began to appear in central Bombay and in the suburbs to serve the middle and occasionally working class students. The older institutions in south Bombay, such as St. Xavier's, Elphinstone, and Government Law College, continued to serve the wealthy upper class. While higher education had been almost exclusively confined to the sons of professionals, wealthy businessmen, and the traditional aristocracy in Bombay, it reached downward to include smaller businessmen and lower level government servants. Admission to college became somewhat easier as the number of seats available was almost doubled. The institutions, however, had no difficulty in finding students for all available places, and educational standards did not suffer seriously.

The development of new colleges was accompanied by an increased emphasis on the existing technological institutions in Bombay. The Victoria Jubilee Technical Institute, one of the oldest such institutions in Asia, was upgraded and expanded. Its student body was particularly active in the political movement and considered itself as something of an elite among the colleges. The Institute of Science also expanded during the 1930's. As educational emphasis shifted from the liberal arts to more technical subjects, there was a change in the kinds of degrees sought by students in Bombay colleges. Prior to 1930 most college students sought degrees in liberal arts, as this constituted the best preparation for the civil service examinations and for further work in law. A small number concentrated on scientific subjects. After 1930, this situation began to change, and larger numbers of students concentrated on scientific subjects.

One of the most important educational issues which aroused the students to action during the 1930's was the question of the matriculation (or secondary school certificate, as they were later called) examinations taken by almost all students at the end of their secondary school career. Criticism of the entire system of examinations goes back almost to the origin of British education in India. Beginning in the 1930's, however, this criticism became quite widespread and vocal. Although some attempts were made to investigate the situation and instigate reforms, the system has remained virtually unchanged to the present time. As early as 1935, a headmaster of a Bombay secondary school wrote in the *Bombay Chronicle* that the system of matriculation examinations was wasteful (since only 20 to 55 per cent passed), harmful to student morale, and unfair.[26] Other critics claimed that the examinations had little relationship to the actual work of the students and that they limited the capabilities of the students and the scope of instruction of the teachers.

Attacks on the matriculation system had been growing for some time, and when the university authorities decided to improve the standard of English in the 1936 examination, thereby raising the level of failures considerably, the students rose in protest. The passing marks fell to 28 per cent, something of a record for Bombay University. The students labelled it a "Matriculation Massacre". Under the leadership of the Students' Brotherhood and the Bombay Students' Union, a series of protest meetings and demonstrations were organized. An *ad hoc* committee was formed, attracting 20,000 students and others.[27] The leaders of the nationalist movement immediately rallied to the side of the students, as did a number of prominent educators. Although under considerable pressure from the public and from the student community, the university authorities felt that the reform which had been instituted was worthwhile, and that a temporary rise in the number of failures was an unfortunate but necessary concomitant.

When the students were convinced that petitions to the proper authorities would not obtain results, mass demonstrations were organized. In June of 1936, a student demonstration of more than 2,000 invaded the meeting of the university senate, demanding that the student leaders be heard and that the matriculation question be reconsidered. When the Senate would not listen to the student demands, the convocation hall was attacked. The student leaders then made speeches until the police forcibly removed them from the hall, arresting a number of students and injuring several.[28]

[26] *Bombay Chronicle*, July 11, 1935, p. 18.
[27] Interview with M. M. Gandhi, Director, Ghia and Company, former student activist, January 22, 1965.
[28] *Bombay Chronicle*, June 16, 1936, p. 7.

The university administration came under heavy attack from the press and from prominent Indian business and educational leaders. The students, meanwhile, kept pressing their campaign, demanding that the passing marks be raised from 29 per cent to 44 per cent, the latter figure being the average of the five preceeding years. As the scope of the demonstrations grew, the students drew up a list of demands which included the following :

1. Reduction of all examination fees.
2. Better facilities for examinations.
3. Appointment of examiners according to merit and not influence.
4. Democratization of the university constitution.
5. No preference to the Cambridge University examination over Indian examinations.
6. Steps to prevent a repetition of the massacre.[29]

Because one of the main instigators of the "massacre" was the British principal of Elphinstone College, the nationalists took advantage of the situation and tried to turn it into an anti-British campaign.

There was no doubt that the percentage of failures in the examination had risen sustantially. In 1931, for example, 57.2 per cent of the students passed the examination, whereas in 1934, only 47.4 per cent passed. The university authorities claimed that the rapid expansion of education had lowered standards to a serious degree and that it was necessary to take steps to raise them before it was too late.[30]

The students were able to win their struggle and, after a long series of demonstrations, the university administration agreed to schedule another examination for those who had failed the first test. The student leaders and the press hailed this as a substantial victory. However, the number passing the supplementary examination was a mere 21 per cent. Several protest meetings were held, but to no avail, and the movement died out.

[29] *Bombay Chronicle*, June 17, 1936, p. 6.
[30] *Bombay Chronicle*, June 12, 1936, p. 9.

The matriculation massacre was one of the first mass student agitations which involved large numbers and used militant tactics. Previously, the nationalist students were unable to convince large numbers of students to commit civil disobedience, although an active minority participated in such activity. A decade of political education and an increasingly political and militant atmosphere in the nation contributed to the students' radicalism. The growth of student political organizations and consciousness during this period was unprecedented, and the major movements on the campus, such as the Congress (nationalist) and the Communist student organizations, were formed at this time.

The matriculation agitation had a number of positive results nevertheless. Not only were the students convinced that they could carry on a successful agitational campaign concerning an academic issue, but a large number of previously uninvolved students were intiated into the student movement. In the long run, the students were successful in the immediate objective of their struggle, since by 1938 the percentage of passes had risen to 53 per cent. They were, however, unable to secure any lasting changes in the system itself.

Occasionally local college issues spurred to action the students at a given institution: One of these incidents took place in 1938, when the Grant Medical College in Bombay announced that all vacations were being cancelled and that other regulations would be strictly observed. The students were quite indignant, and when representations to the Health Minister proved ineffective, they resorted to a strike which was completely effective. The incident was limited to the Grant Medical College, although it did receive a good deal of publicity and aroused the sympathy of students at other institutions. The agitation included protest meetings as well as a strike. The school's administration tried to compromise with the students, although most of the new regulations were kept in force. This is only one example of many similar incidents which took place during the 1930's. As the students became aware that agitational methods could often gain results, they resorted to such tactics with increasing regularity. Since much of the student movement was more interested in political issues than in educational reform, they were more than willing to participate in demonstrations and agitational campaigns which might embarrass the authorities and thereby help the nationalist causes. The usual pattern was a short strike, which usually emptied the college in question, followed by sporadic demonstrations and ending in a surrender by the students, although sometimes a compromise was reached with the administration of the college.

Not all of the student activity during this period was devoted to politics. The agitations concerning the matriculation massacre indicate that educational issues also roused the students to action. Of less dramatic impact, though perhaps of more importance were the other student activities sponsored by a range of groups. To obtain a complete picture of the student situation in Bombay during the 1930's, it is necessary to examine these social and cultural activities, as well as those concerned with agitation and politics. There was a mixture of politics in many of the social and cultural activities of this period, indicating that complete divorce from the events of the outside world was impossible for the students.

During the entire period of the Thirties, such groups as the Young Men's Hindu Association, the Young Men's Parsi Association, the Marwari Youth League, and the Muslim Students' Union were meeting actively. The usual pattern of activity was to sponsor a series of four to six lectures each academic year and to hold several social gatherings. Most of these communal social groups received the guidance and assistance of influential adults in the community. Most of them were not at all involved in student political activities, although the nationalst student groups ried to extend their influence into as many other organizations as possilble.

Occasionally, one of the student organizations made specific suggestions for educational reforms. In 1935, the University Reform League issued a statement which said:

> A university is primarily a community of students. The true spirit of the university lies in the corporate life which the students live in their pursuit of learning and in acquiring the experience of life.[31]

[31] *Bombay Chronicle*, December 2, 1935, p. 5.

Some of the League's suggestions for changes were:

1. Formation of Students' Brotherhoods in all educational centers with library, games and gym.
2. Nomination by the chancellor of one or two students to the senate annually.
3. Study by students of the history of their college in order to develop pride.
4. Investigation of student living conditions.[32]

Later a delegation of students went to the vice chancellor in order to urge the university to undertake social service work. The students asked that a literacy campaign in the slums of Bombay be officially sponsored by the university. The vice chancellor, fearing to take part in an activity which might appear to be political, declined and called the students subversive.[33] Other student groups, in addition to the nationalist organizations, engaged in social service work.

Athletic activity also proved fairly pouular among students. Many of the colleges sponsored athletic teams, with cricket as the most popular sport. The communal student groups also had active sports programs, and the annual competitions between some of the colleges attracted a good deal of attention. The university, and most of the colleges, suffered from a lack of facilities for sports and of sufficient space for games, but attempts were made to provide opportunities. In the late 1930's, some of the communal groups, such as the militant Hindu R.S.S., began to use athletic training and drill as part of a nationalistic or communalistic training program. Throughout the perio, however, athletic activity involved many students and provided one of the few outlets for physical exercise open to young people.

Some students cultural and social activities played an important political role. One of the places set aside for student social gatherings in Bombay was the R. L. Trust Hostel. Donated by a prominent industrialist with strong nationalist leanings, the Hostel had a good library and several meeting rooms.

---

[32] *Ibid.*, p. 6.
[33] Interview with Dr. Aloo Dastur, Head of the Department of Politics, University of Bombay, January 8, 1965.

It was located, moreover, in a neighborhood about equally distant from the newer colleges and the established institutions of South Bombay. The Hostel developed into a center of meeting and discussion for the more radical elements in the Bombay student community. Informal study circles were organized, and serious discussions were held. The students invited well known political leaders to the Hostel to talk to them and even succeeded in sponsoring several underground leaders. Many of the alumni of this study group are active in political affairs in present day India.

Conclusion

The period under consideration in this chapter is of particular importance for the student movement in Bombay and in India. Not only did the movement transform itself dramatically from a campus based movement interested essentially in national issues into an important arm of the nationalist movement, but developed a mass base and organizational and political sophistication. The student movement adjusted to the changes in the educational system in Bombay, and after a short period of confusion, succeeded in organizing the middle class students from the newer colleges. Student organizations which had previously been interested in politics and occasionally active in political affairs, transformed themselves into militant political movements.

The student movement received the active support and encouragement from the leaders of the various political groups in India. For its part, the student movement also influenced the adult organizations to a more modest extent. Student meetings often passed resolutions urging the Congress to take more radical stands, and leftist Congress leaders pointed to this evidence of student opinion. The student movement was an integral part of the national movement and played a vital role in it.[31]

The integral relationship between the political organizations and the student movement during this period is clear. Political activists were able to work within the student movement mainly because of the dramatic mass movement which had captured the imagination of much of the student population.

[34] Interview with Ramesh Sanghvi, foreign editor, *Blitz*, March 16, 1965.

The students were among the strongest supporters of left-wing nationalist leaders, and the student movement was probably the most left-wing of the elements supporting the Congress. Because of the political situation in India and the more modern and Western orientation of the students, ideological politics, and particularly socialist ideas, had a good deal of popularity on the campuses.

The political parties were able to recruit leadership from the campuses, and many of the student leaders who left the colleges for active politics became leaders of Bombay politics after Independence. The Congress (and the Communists as well) could often count on the students for active political workers in the trade union movement and in other areas. The ideological basis which the students received in the student movement made them particularly effective in broader political endeavors. Thus, the relationship between campus and the political groups was close and quite important.

Some contemporary observers saw the student movement in Bombay as the leading element in the Indian student movement at the time. The Bombay students were not only at the center of political activity in India, but the headquarters of the political student organizations were in Bombay. The Bombay students had a contact with student organizations in Europe and the United States and were quite internationally minded. They were quite disturbed by the Spanish Civil War and by the Japanese invasion of China. These international contacts helped to broaden the perspective of the student leaders.[35]

Some have seen the period between 1936 and 1940 as the apex of the student movement in India. In urban areas, the students were able to obtain mass support, while student organizations began to develop in provincial areas, an unprecedented development.[36] The fact that the Bombay Students' Union claimed a membership of 5,000 when the total college population in the city was about 20,000 is significant.

It was during the period under consideration that the students of Bombay learned the fundamentals of agitational politics and of the organization of mass movements. It has

---

[35] Interview with Pohekar, *loc. cit.*
[36] Reddy, *op. cit.*, p. 131.

been said that the period was marked by a sense of nationalism coupled with socialist idealism".[37] These two potent ideological trends, although diluted by factional strugges, proved as volatile in India among the students as in many other parts of the world. Certainly the ideological concerns of this period were one of the hallmarks of the student movement. If anything, the students were more concerned with matters of ideology than were the adult movements of the times, and took these considerations more seriously. An adult leader stated that "the discussions and fiery speeches of the [Bombay Presidency Students'] Conference only reminded one of the debating societies either at Oxford or Cambridge".[38] Many of the present political intellectuals in India, men like M. R. Masani, Ashoka Mehta, R. M. Lohia, S. M. Joshi, S. A. Dange, and P. C. Joshi, on all sides of the political spectrum, have come from the student movement and received much of their early ideological training in the movement.

Little has been said in this chapter about the role of the student movement in influencing or determining educational policies or its role in university politics. The reason for this apparent omission is relatively simple—the students did not take much interest in these matters as they were too much involved in broader political concerns. Student interest in educational issues was generally limited to those relatively minor agitational campaigns which could add to the nationalist conflict.

The leadership of the student movement remained in the hands of the "elite"—both intellectual elite and class/caste elite in the colleges. While higher education was beginning to change and the student population included more representatives from the lower middle and working classes, the student organizations, both political and non-political, remained the almost exclusive preserves of upper caste and class elements. There seemed to be no significant difference between the leadership characteristics of the various kinds of organizations, although the political movement naturally had more activist leaders. The political organizations also had a high status,

[37] Ahluwalia, *op. cit.*, p. 40.
[38] *Bombay Chronicle*, January 7, 1937, p. 7.

and active cadres were respected for their involvement, as well as for their scholastic achievement.

It would be a mistake to assume that the entire attention of the campus was turned to the political struggle. On the contrary, during lulls in agitational campaigns, college life was normal, with the large majority of the student population concerned with political issues only during times of acute crisis. The various cultural and socal organizations continued much as before, and while the students were more aware of politics than ever before, they were not preoccupied or even primarily concerned with the nationalist struggle. Thus, a student movement at its zenith of activity and strength was still unable to permanently transform the campus, and despite its ability to create chaos in higher education, it was never able to obtain the full support of the student population.

The student movement of the 1930's shows the maximum effects of a value and societal orientation of the student movement. As will be seen, the total neglect of educational issues and concerns has had repercussions on the student movement in later periods, and the pattern for intense political and ideological activity was set during the 1930's. So strong was this trend in student organiatzions and attitudes, that it proved impossible to break when it no longer served the needs of the student population and was not practical as a basis for student organization.

CHAPTER V

THE STUDENT AS POLITICAL ACTIVIST— THE 1942 MOVEMENT

THE INDIAN struggle for independence extended over a period of almost two decades of intermittent conflict. Its height came in 1942, when India approached revolution. The movement led by Gandhi and the Indian National Congress differed significantly from other anti-colonial uprisings because of its stress on non-violent tactics. However, the Indian National Congress only occasionally threatened the British administration. Because the "Quit India" campaign of 1942 was one of the few times that the nationalist movement came close to achieving its political goals, it is a particularly important aspect of recent Indian history.

In 1942, Bombay found itself in the center of the "Quit India" campaign. The campaign started after the meeting of the All-India Congress Committee in Bombay in August of 1942. Most Congress leaders were arrested in Bombay immediately after the meeting, and in the midst of city-wide demonstrations and riots, the students emerged as a leading element of the entire effort.

When the All-India Congress Committee issued its call for mass action to expel the British from the sub-continent, the student movement was ready to take part. In early August of 1942, the All-India Congress Committee, after having lost faith in British promises of increased self-government for India and with the recent Cripps mission, issued a ringing statement urging Indians to "do or die" and demanding that the British "Quit India" before India would fight for the Allies in the Second World War. Indians were urged to resist the British in every possible way, short of outright violence. The Congress asked for an open, though non-violent, rebellion against the British. The nationalist movement responded enthusiastically to the call, the various kinds of civil disobedience immediately began to occur throughout India.

The overwhelming political orientation of the major student groups had built up a militancy among the student cadres. For more than five years, the student groups had concentrated on political issues, both educational and agitational, and the previous emphasis on educational concerns had been all but forgotten by most students. The fact that the 1942 campaign was so successful on the campuses is probably due to a combination of this intense organizational effort and the excitement of the nationalist movement in the broader society.

The radical student groups, in particular, had been conducting study classes and preparing their members for active political combat.

Perhaps at no other time have Indian students been so value-oriented in their political views, and so able to relate ideological issues to a militant war of national liberation. The students who were involved in a continuing movement saw the relationship of the student political organizations and broader issues in society. The movement, for example, was very active in social work and in the labor movement, thereby giving evidence of their broader political concern.

There were substantial segments of the Indian population which were actively opposed to the "Quit India" movement. The Indian Communist Party strongly supported the British war effort as an important fight against fascism, which in their view necessarily came before the fight for India's independence. Communist influenced organizations such as the All-India Trade Union Congress, the All-India Kisan Sabha (peasants' organization), the Peoples' Theater, the Communist All-India Students' Federation, and other cultural and political groups also opposed the Congress during this time.

The Communists found themselves in a difficult position during this period. In the student movement, for instance, many Communist students who were as much nationalist as Marxist resigned from the party and were valuable additions to the nationalist camp. Similar occurences took place in the other Communist front organizations, as well as in the Party itself. The "Peoples' War" line which the Communists followed during this period may have served the needs of the Soviet Union and the international Communist movement, but was certainly an ineffective policy in the light of the political situation in India. The Communists had the advantage of British support during this period. While nationalist leaders were placed in prison and their organizations declared illegal, the Communists who had been in jail were released. Communist organizations functioned without interference from the British.

The Muslim students, who were fairly well organized at this time, did not take part in the nationalist struggle. The Muslim League, which had captured the affiliations of most Muslims in Bombay, maintained a generally neutral attitude toward the events of 1942. Naturally, the minority of Congress oriented Muslims did take an active part in the struggle, and a number of them went to jail for their activities. However, the largest Muslim organization, the Bombay Presidency Muslim Students' Federation, remained neutral in the anti-British campaigns, and the Muslim Students' Union, although nominally under nationalist control, remained silent as well as did the right-wing Hindu oriented R.S.S.

Student Organizations and the "Quit India" Movement

The organization of the student movement in Bombay during the 1942 struggle was not too difficult to comprehend. The most active elements of the student movement at this time, were, naturally, the nationalist organizations. The nationalist segment of the Bombay Students' Union (later to become the Students' Congress could depend upon two or three thousand active members at this time; 1,000 students were involved in the dangerous underground movement.[1] At Elphinstone College the nationalists had at least 100 active workers and attracted 1,000 students to various demonstrations, indicating the strength of the movement in the "prestige" colleges of the city. At other colleges, the number of active workers was probably smaller, although still substantial.[2] St. Xavier's College had about fifty activists; the other colleges in Bombay had a similar number. According to one observer, "more than 80 per cent of the students [in Bombay] participated in the strug-

[1] Interview with Sushil Jhaveri, former activist, Students' Congress, March 2, 1965.
[2] Interview with Dr. G. G. Parikh, Secretary of the Praja Socialist Party, Bombay, December 12, 1964.

gle".[3] This estimate is probably somewhat high, although the level of participation was clearly unprecedented.

Although the constituent branches of the Bombay Students' Union elected representatives to a central working committee, the organization was characterized by its autonomy. In most instances, the students in each college or area chose their own projects. When students leaders were arrested, the working committee usually called for an received a one day strike in all the colleges and schools of the city. The liaison between the adult nationalist leadership and the students was very strategic at this time. The students provided a key contact between the underground nationalist leadership and the outside world.[4] During much of the period that the top leaders of the Congress in Bombay were in prison, students actually led the nationalist forces in the city, often with a good deal of political sophistication. The adult leadership found it necessary to depend upon the students, not only for manpower in demonstrations but for co-ordination and some leadership.

The North Bombay Students' Union, one of the most active segments of the student movement in Bombay, illustrates the operation of the movement at this time. The N.B.S.U. was controlled by the Communists until 1942, when most of the leadership transferred its allegiance to the Congress. The intensely political background of the leaders in the N.B.S.U. explains why they approached the nationalist struggle with such political sophistication. It is estimated that there were about 400 activists in the N.B.S.U.[5] The main focus of the N.B.S.U.'s activity was national politics; there was little interest in campus issues. While study circles were continued by the organization, attendance was poor as students were more interested in a directly agitational program than in the theoretical aspects of the struggle. During the height of the 1942 offensive, the North Bombay Students' Union had a membership of about 10,000.[6]

[3] Pravina Mehta, "Observations, in Retrospect, on the Indian Nationalis Movement" (unpublished paper, University of Chicago, 1951), p. 5.
[4] Interview with Raja Kulkarni, former Secretary of the North Bombay Students' Union, March 13, 1965.
[5] Interview with Phatak, *loc. cit.*
[6] Interview with Kulkarni, *loc. cit.*

The Communist student movement found that the 1942 movement placed severe strains on its organization and membership. As one observer has noted, Communist organizations lost less support during 1942 than would have been the case were they not free to organize while the Congress leaders were behind bars.[7] As a result, the Communist journal *The Student* claimed that 1,500 new members had been enrolled in the Communist student organizations. The report went on to state, however, that 1,500 was not a large figure in view of the fact that at least 5,000 students had become politically conscious in Bombay in the previous several months.[8]

When the line had been changed, the Communists actively opposed the Congress; despite substantial odds against them, Communist students attempted to break up nationalist meetings and to persuade students to stay in their classes. Several meetings were called to protest acts of sabotage which the nationalist movement had committed. While the Communists wanted to divert the attention of the students to social service and educational projects far removed from the anti-British campaigns, the nationalists attached the Communists as unpatriotic. It was not uncommon for Communist students to be attacked in the steets of Bombay.

Both the Communist and nationalist student organizations had the same name at this time, the Bombay Students' Union, and as a result organizational differentiation was often difficult. Nevertheless, the efforts of the Communist section of the Bombay Students' Union to redirect the student movement to campus issues and to interest the students in educational questions failed, and the student movement remained politically oriented.

Although the main focus of the nationlist student movement in 1942 was on the political struggle, there was a substantial amount of non-political activity as well. It is a little known fact that the the Indian National Theater, which has achieved national fame and some international renown in post-Independence India, was born out of the student movement. Student

---

[7] Interview with P. C. Joshi, former Secretary of the Communist Party of India, January 12, 1965.

[8] *The Student* (Bombay), January, 1943, p. 8.

leaders, interested both in dramatics and in countering the influence of the Communists-dominated Peoples' Theater movement, started the Indian National Theater in 1942.[9] In its early days, the majority of its actors were students, although as the idea of nationalist oriented dramatic organization took hold, others became interested in the I.N.T., and it gradually outgrew its student founders and became professionalised in 1949. The Theater itself and student groups under the auspices of the I.N.T. toured villages and smaller towns, portraying the nationalist message through the medium of drama.

After August 9, 1942 when the Congress called for its "do or die" campaign, the students began a strike which closed virtually all of the colleges and most of the schools in Bombay for three months. Nationalist students forcibly prevented students who were not interested in politics or who were Communists from entering the institutions. Force was rarely needed, though, for it was clear that the vast majority of the student community supported the strike, if only because it provided an extended vacation. On several occasions, students destroyed college property and went into the streets breaking street lights and government property. By and large, however, the agitations and strikes proceeded without incident, and most college principals closed their institutions promptly, not wishing to court violence. There were few expulsions because of participation in these strikes; even recognized student leaders were seldom taken to task by the college authorities.

In recognition of the power of the student agitations, Bombay University ordered the term ended two weeks ahead of schedule to minimize the effects of the strikes.[10] Students also boycotted the final examinations at a number of institutions. At the Victoria Jubilee Technical Institute 15 out of 212 students attended the final examinations.[11] The colleges in Bombay finally reopened on November 3, 1942, and attendance was fairly normal. Isolated strikes continued to take place in Bombay. These strikes, and particularly the general strike which closed the schools for four months, gave the students a sense of their power, and

---

[9] Interview with Jhaveri, *loc. cit.*
[10] *Bombay Chronicle*, September 18, 1942, p. 8.
[11] *Bombay Chronicle*, October 9, 1942, p. 3.

of the effectiveness of the strike as a weapon in the fight for independence.

In addition to the traditional educational activities and agitation of the student movement, students were involved in more dangerous projects during the 1942 struggle. The leftist Congress leaders, many of whom were able to go underground before the British could arrest them, called on the students to provide assistance to the nationalist leadership. During 1942, the students organized their own underground movement, which involved more than 1,000 students in the Bombay area.[12] A tightly controlled organizational structure insured that tasks were carried out efficiently. A number of politically active student leaders also went underground during this period, guiding the student movement by means of secret messages and other conspirational methods. A substantial percentage of those students who were involved in the movement eventually saw the inside of a jail cell, since security arrangements were lax and police spies were everywhere.

One observer has noted that "the underground movement of young men and women continued paralyzing the Government machinery" during the struggle.[13] Students arranged public meetings, printed, duplicated, and distributed illegal Congress bulletins and pamphlets, maintained communications between underground leaders and the open Congress movement, collected news, and attended to families of jailed Congress workers.[14]

In addition to the administrative tasks of conducting a movement harassed by British authorities, the underground movement was also interested in distrupting British administration as as much as possible. To this end, sabotage activities were carried out by the students, aimed at thwarting the British administration in India. Although not in the spirit of Gandhian nonviolence, the students claimed that Gandhi had asked people to participate in the best way they know. Nevertheless, sabotage activity, which reached substantial proportions, was never officially sponsored by any of the Congress organizations, although Congressmen were responsible for such activity.

[12] Interview with Jhaveri, *loc. cit.* p. 85.
[13] Govind Sahai, *The '42 Rebellion* (Delhi: Rajkamal Publications, 1947).
[14] Interview with Jhaveri, *loc. cit.*

The sabotage activity took a number of different forms during the 1942 struggle. College property was one object of sabotage activity. At Ismail Yusuf College, in a suburb of Bombay, a student was arrested for stealing chemicals for explosives from the laboratory. During November, bombs exploded at Wilson and Elphinstone Colleges, doing substantial damage. In September of 1942, a number of trains were damaged by homemade bombs. At the *Times of India,* the leading pro-British nepspaper in India, one press was damaged and a large quantity of paper destroyed by saboteurs. Several attempts were made to set fire to the main post office in Bombay by mailing bombs concealed in packages. While none of these attempts was successful, several district post offices and a large quantity of mail were destroyed. In the countryside, students were engaged in ripping up railroad tracks, destroying telegraph communications; they tried to create a guerilla movement which could live off the land for sustained periods of time. Much of the sabotage work was completely uncoordinated, and almost all of it was committed by the students. However, while the British were inconvenienced by the sabotage, they were never seriously threatened by it.

One of the most interesting aspects of the underground segment of the 1942 struggle was the secret Congress Radio which broadcast to the Bombay area from August to November of 1942. The idea for the clandestine radio station came from a group of nationalist students in a Congress sponsored Hindi teaching program. Several underground leaders, such as Ram Manohar Lohia and Smt. Sucheta Kripalani, provided guidance to the students.

The entire radio scheme was operated by ten people who were responsible for the technical aspects as well as the programming of the Congress Radio. The radio broadcast only half an hour per day, and it was necessary to evade the British authorities by moving the transmitter frequently.

The Congress Radio was eventually discovered by the police through a Bombay radio dealer. Five of the key organizers were imprisoned, several for periods of up to four years. The Congress Radio was one of the most exciting aspects of the student movement during this period, succeeding in catching the imagination of many people.[15]

Students in Prison

Jails have traditionally played an important role in the development of revolutionary student movements. India is no exception, for many well known nationalist leaders received their training in British jails. The Bombay student movement owes its existence, in no small measure, to the British prison system in India. With the larger number of students in prisons during the 1942 struggle, the jails became an important center of political activity.

Students had been in and out of jails ever since the beginning of the civil disobedience movement in 1930. Even prior to that time, students involved in the terrorist movement spent a number of years in prison, P. C. Joshi, a noted Indian Communist, has stated that "jails make Communists" and that many of the nationalist terrorists who were jailed in the 1920's were converted to communism while in prison.[16] The group of young people who had been ideologically trained in the jails provided a number of the early leaders of the All-India Students' Federation. In those early days, prison study circles were organized, and such authors as Trotsky, the Webbs, and other leftists were avidly read by the students. These books were usually smuggled into the jails. The efforts of the Communists within the jails were particularly effective, and a real sense of community was built up on the basis of those intense study circles.[17] On several occasions, the student political prisoners led other inmates in protesting against bad prison conditions; however, in most cases, students had no complaint with conditions, and the British allowed them a sufficient amount of freedom within the jails. Prisoners with terms of a year or more were often able to learn an additional language in jail, in keeping with Gandhi's desire that all Indians learn the national language, Hindustani.

[15] Pravina Mehta, "Observations in Retrospect...", *op. cit.*, p. 5.
[16] Interview with Joshi, *loc. cit.*
[17] Interview with M. M. Gandhi, *loc. cit.*

During the 1942 movement students demonstrated against inadequate prison conditions and facilities; their grievances were met. Congress workers organized study classes in Bombay's Worli jail, which housed the bulk of the students arrested in 1942. They encountered no interference by the prison authorities, who were glad that the Congress prisoners were occupying themselves. A number of the adult socialists in jail took responsibility for the classes, which included discussions of Marx and classical economists, prospects for Indian independence, and other political issues. Student leaders also spent much time in planning their activities after their release from prison, and blueprints of student agitational campaigns were developed in the jails.[18] Specific plans were made for the operation of the Indian National Theater, which later became an important cultural institution in India. As Gandhi himself said, the jail was the university for the students of the nationalist movement.

Many of the student leaders look back with fondness on their experiences in jail. The community built up in the jails was convivial, and many of the alumni of the 1942 movement have kept up contacts. Prison life allowed sufficient time for study and reflection as well as the discussions which were so important to the political and social development of many of the participants.

Conclusion

The 1942 movement itself was of a substantial scope. On the national scene during the 1942 movement 60,229 people were arrested, 940 were killed by the police or army, and about 25,000 were injured. Three hundred and eighteen police stations were destroyed, and telephone lines were cut in 12,000 places.[19] In Maharashtra alone 8,225 people were arrested during the struggle. During the first part of the struggle, the whole city of Bombay was in chaos, and a general strike engulfed the city for several days.

[18] Interview with Parikh, *loc. cit.*
[19] Sahai, *op. cit.*, p. 21.

A contemporary account gives a feeling for the nature and scope of the activity at that time:

> As students we were busy organizing the general students body toward active participation in the daily demonstrations. All meetings being banned, we met in secret. Each meeting came out with the program for the day following, one day it would be the picketing of the Stock Market, or a procession around the city which would start at many places and meet at a given point to repeat the August Resolution (of the Congress); the next might be a public meeting under the guise of prayer in a temple courtyard where we would distribute our literature. As the time passed repression increased and more and more people were jailed. The student leaders were being victimized every day in the colleges and before I was asked to leave school, I left of my own account, as I was too busy with agitation to attend classes and as my agitation consisted in part of persuading others to leave classes. The repercussions frightened some students into inaction and we devised many ways to get these people to co-operate in some small way, such as making hand painted posters and putting them up at night around their neighborhood. We also conducted demonstrations in the primary and high schools, one very effective means which I remmember was the "its a lie" program which exposed the British rewriting of history in Indian schools.
>
> The end of my activities came after I had been several times arrested and finally jailed. At this time my mother had become inactive in the movement, but when I was jailed I met her there, as she had also been arrested for carrying a flag on a sudden impulse. I was tried in court and sentenced to two months for contempt of court. Two months in jail was not without activity, and we continued demonstrations and protests, such as hunger strikes and hoisting national flags.[20]

The official historical record of the University of Bombay also stated that the demonstrations of 1942 seriously disrupted the

[20] Pravina Mehta, "Observations in Retrospect....", *op. cit.*, p. 12.

activity of the university.[21]

The response of students to the 1942 movement has several causes. 1942 was the height of the nationalist struggle in India, and its implications could hardly escape any urban Indian. Politics was not abstract, and although it was the concern of only a relatively small minority, it succeeded in galvanizing India's cities as no social movement had before or has since. For perhaps the first time a movement had substantial mass support. The nationalist and Communist student movements had done almost a decade of spadework, and had built up a substantial number of active and sophisticated student workers. The **Bombay Chronicle** saw the movement as the culmination of several decades of political training of the student movement, and it praised the role of the students in the struggle.[22] The adult political movements did their best to involve students in politics and recruit students for their activities. The students themselves felt that they had a legitimate role to play in politics.

The nationalist student movement also had its first taste of political power and influence during the 1942 movement. These student leaders, with little previous political experience, were able to take substantial responsibilities for the operation of the entire nationalist movement. By and large, they executed their tasks with distinction. The period also indicated the strength of the left-wing on the student movement. While Gandhi was universally respected in India, Nehru and the other socialist leaders were popular among the students. The enthusiastic response of the students to the sabotage efforts of a section of the nationalist movement showed that the ideas of Gandhian non-violence were not strong among them.

The leadership of the movement during this period remained fixed among the middle and upper middle class students; the major leaders attended the prestige colleges in South Bombay.[23] Most of these leaders had been trained in the study circles and other educational activities of the political parties, although a

[21] S. R. Dongerkery, *A History of the University of Bombay* (Bombay: University of Bombay Press,, 1957), p. 320.
[22] *Bombay Chronicle*, November 3, 1942, p. 4.
[23] Interview with Jhaveri, *loc. cit.*

few spontaneous leaders did develop in the course of the struggle. As in the past, most of the student leaders came from financially stable families, though a minority came from the elite of the city. By all accounts, Maharashtrians were involved in sabotage and other underground activities to a greater extend that Gujaratis; there was a sprinkling of students from the minority communities in the movement. For the first time, however, the newer schools of North Bombay and the suburban areas were very much involved in the movement and developed their own indigenous leadership.

The 1942 movement shows the student organizations at the height of their value-oriented period. Campus and other educational issues were totally subordinated to political affairs, at a time when ideological consciousness of the student community was very high. For many students, the political struggle meant more than their whole academic careers; many students who willingly left college proved this fact.

The most lasting significance of the 1942 movement was probably its effects on the students rather than their effect on broader areas of national politics. The struggle provided student leaders with lessons in politics and to the rank and file a sense of political participation. The vivid memories which former leaders have of their participation in the movement and existence of a group of "1942" alumni" are indications of the value of this period.

CHAPTER VI

STUDENTS AND INDEPENDENCE (1943-1947)

THE "Quit India" movement which was started by the Congress in 1942 could not sustain its momentum, and the revolutionary upsurge which the Congress had hoped would drive the British from the sub-continent did not develop. The arrest of the nationalist leadership, the intensification of police harassment, and the inability of the nationalists to involve the rural masses meant that the 1942 movement could not succeed in achieving the goal of national independence. The movement for independence did, however, continue until the British agreed to grant India her freedom in 1947. Indian political patterns continued to develop, and many which were established during this final period of the independence movement have persisted to the present time.

The period from 1943 to 1947 was also a marked contrast to the immediately preceding period in that the struggle was not a continuous threat to the British, but was a sporadic agitational movement which, with the excepion of the brief naval mutiny in 1946, constituted no serious threat to British rule in India. Much of the militancy of the previous period was lost, and by 1944 there was every reason for the British to expect that the crisis in India had ended.

The Congress had to pay a price for the change in organization from a militant movement for national liberation to a committed but less idealistic political party. This price became evident during the 1943-47 period when Congress began to lose its mass following and its image of unquestionable integrity. The Indian masses, and particularly the working classes in the cities and towns, began to lose interest in politics as the clear and simple appeals of Mahatma Gandhi were replaced by complex and often conflicting statements from political leaders.

The loss of mass following during the mid-1940's and the internal dissension within the movement had a predictably disillusioning influence on those activists who had joined the movement to achieve independence and who were uninterested in internal political feuds or in theoretical ideological issues. The inability of the students to sustain a mass agitational movement caused some disillusionment also. The main cause for discontent was the changing political situation in India. The issue was no longer simply one of active opposition to British rule, for, as 1947 approached, the Congress leadership had to concern itself with the mundane but highly important matter of the transfer of power. Compromise with the British, the Muslim League, Indian business interests, and other groups was the order of the day.

Bombay colleges returned to normal in 1943. The student movement was still firmly entrenched in most of the colleges, and both Communist and Congress organizations existed in many high schools. The Muslim student groups also attracted substantial numbers and the militant Hindu R.S.S. was quite active among the students. Despite this activity, however, the student movement was never able to sustain the level of agitational activity which characterized it in the 1942 movement. The level of agitational activity fell perceptibly; at no time were all of the colleges on strike for a sustained period as they had been in 1942. Simultaneously, student organizations began to concentrate more on campus-oriented issues, although campus agitations were often directly linked to political issues.

Students and Politics: Nationalists Versus Communists

During the crisis of the 1942 struggle, the leadership of the nationalist student movement had little time to concern itself with the confusing state of Bombay student organizations. The existence of two separate Bombay Students' Unions, each with widely divergent political views, was both confusing and detrimental to the nationalist cause. Neither group wished to relinquish the reputation and tradition of the organization's name, especially the Communists, whose reputation had suffered greatly with the commencement of the "Peoples' War" line. When the pressure of agitational activities abated somewhat, the leadership of the nationalist student movement in Bombay had an opportunity to correct this confusing situation.

One of the major themes of the Communist movement during this period was that of student unity. The Communists' main interest was probably in ending their isolation from the mainstream of the movement; the unity theme was therefore a useful tool. Consequently, both sides continually stressed the importance of unity in the student movement; yet, both continued their divergent policies. Partially in response to a Communist propaganda offensive in favor of student unity, the nationalist student groups called a Students' Unity Conference in August of 1943.

Nationalist students (a combination of socialists and Gandhians) invited all student factions in Bombay to atteed the conference, realizing that their invitation would probably be rejected by those students who opposed the nationalist stand. It appeared doubtful from the outset that the Unity Conference could in any way further true unity among the different camps.

The conference itself was well organized and well attended. According to the *Hind-Praja*, a radical student journal,

> August 21, 1943 was a historical day in the history of the student movement in the city. Workers of the North Bombay Students' Union and the Bombay Students' Union had organized a Unity Conference which was attended by about 3,000 students. The conference, which was of course a grand success, laid down a new political line, a new organizational policy, and a program. A Unity Committee was formed and our union began to function according to the program of the Unity Committee[1]

A number of resolutions were passed which were to form the ideological basis for the student movement in Bombay for the next several years. Their resolution on Russia and China was a challenge to the Communist student movement, unequivocally stating the nationalist position on the war. It read:

> The Conference of students of Bombay express their deep sympathy and accord their warmest greetings to the brave youth of Russia and China who have fought and are fighting their wars

[1] *Hind-Praja*, October 1943, p. 10.

of national liberation against the forces of aggression. The students of India feel that India's struggle for freedom against British imperialism is also a part of the world's struggle against all aggression. We hope that we will soon be able to march with other progressive forces towards the common idea.[2]

The most important document of the conference was the "Student Unity Manifesto". In its preamble, the manifesto stated:

This Unity Manifesto was originally drawn up in the Worli Jail where all the student workers were undergoing imprisonment. After the release of many of the student workers in June last, they decided to carry further the work of uniting the different organizations and sections of the students. This conference was the result of their work.[3]

The manifesto took a strongly nationalist tone, and called for the divergent student organizations in Bombay to unite under the banner of the Committee. Nevertheless, if the conference is to be judged on the basis of its success in uniting the student movement in Bombay, it was a total failure. However, neither the organizers nor the participants expected real unity to take pace. The conference was mainly intended to coordinate and integrate the nationalist student movement which emerged from the 1942 struggle.

Many students wavering between the Communists and nationalists were drawn into the nationalist movement as a result of the conference. Furthermore, the conference formed a continuing organizational structure to take the place of the nationalist Bombay Students' Union. A Students' Unity Committee was set up to coordinate all of the student activities in Bombay, including representatives of the various student groups and factions. However, from the beginning the Committee was dominated by the socialists, with the cooperation of the Gandhians. The formation of the Committee did clarify the student situation, however, for there were now two major organizations:

[2] *Ibid.*
[3] *Ibid.*, p. 2.

the Unity Committee, dominated by the nationalists, and the Bombay Students' Union, controlled by the Communists.

The Communists, for their part, kept firm control over the Bombay Students' Union, which continued in its affiliation with the All-India Students' Federation. The Muslims were active in the Bombay Presidency Muslim Students' Federation, which espoused the position of the Muslim League. The Hindu right-wing-controlled R.S.S. was without a specifically student wing, although it did involve many students in its programs. Along side these political or semi-political organizations, a number of cultural and social groups continued to exist, although those did not attract as much attention or support as did the more active groups.

The stabilization of the student groups in Bombay did not cause an end to the conflicts between student organizations. The most graphic instance of these disputes occurred when a large number of nationalist students attacked the offices of the Communist dominated Bombay Students' Union and tried to gain control by force of the files and records of the organization. These disturbances ceased when the police arrested six students and the organization was evicted from the premises by the worried landlord. Communists were labeled as "traitors", and strong propaganda campaigns were conducted against them by the nationalists. In their efforts to recruit members, both factions in the student movement bitterly attacked each other in the press and at meetings, and efforts to mediate this dispute failed.[4] The conflict alienated many students from both groups.

The invective between the various factions of the student movement persisted up to and after Independence. Gandhi was moved in 1944 to state:

> Power politics should be unknown to the student world. Immediately (when) they dabble in that class of work, there ceases to be a students' will, (and) therefore they fail to serve the country in its time of crisis.[5]

[4] Interview with Pravina Mehta, *loc. cit.*
[5] K. Diraviyam, "Whither the Student Movement", *Sathi*, June 1, 1946, p. 3.

By 1946, political factions, from the Communists and socialists to the smaller splinter groups such as the Revolutionary Socialist Party and the Forward Bloc, were concentrating much attention on the student movement. Full time party workers went among the students to build political organizations. Many students interested in a national non-party movement opposed this tendency, although there was little they could do to counteract it. The official Congress organization, in contrast, paid little attention to the student movement; consequently, they lost much of the support they had amassed in 1942 among the students.[6]

Since the student movement had been directed almost exclusively toward the goal of independence, the end of the "revolutionary" period of the nationalist movement meant the loss of a substantial part of the students *raison d'etre* for political participation. The broader political groups, at the same time, found it necessary to build up maximum support in preparation for national elections and the Indian constitutional convention. The political parties simply had insufficient resources to devote to the students, and they made a virtue of necessity by urging students to remain aloof from politics. The *raison d-etre* of the movement remained national political issues, although campus issues were reintroduced. The sabotage effort continued; both Grant Medical College and Sydenham College were damaged by bombs. When Professor P. A. Wadia was ousted from Wilson College for his outspoken pro-nationalist views, the students called a strike and launched an agitational program that resulted in the suspension of eighty students. Students at Wilson College, G. S. Medical College and other institutions collected a substantial amount of money to aid the victims of the 1943 Bengal famine. All student groups cooperated on this project; Communist student organizations sent several teams of students to Bengal to do social service work and to distribute food which was donated by the Bombay students.

Nationalist students served as volunteer workers in the Congress campaign for the 1943 municipal elections during

[6] Interview with Chandrakant Dalal, former Treasurer, All-India Students' Congress, March 20, 1965.

which violence between nationalist students and pro-Muslim League elements was comomn. The Congress candidates were successful in the election, a fact which bolstered the students' feeling of political influence. Nationalist students set up a Political Sufferers Relief Fund, designed to aid families of imprisoned Congress workers. The students staged cultural programs and collected funds in the streets. On the annual "Suffers Day" in 1944, for instance, Rs. 25,000 was collected.[7] As a part of their social service program Communist student organizations placed particular stress on constructive work. This emphasis was undertaken as part of a political program aimed at undermining the support of the Congress at a crucial period. By diverting the attention of the students from politics, the Communists reasoned, the nationalist movement would be weekened and at the same time constructive work would be done. When an explosion on a dock in Bombay caused tremendous damage to the surrounding working class area, the student movement took the initiative in providing immediate assistance. The socialist volunteer group, the Rashtra Seva Dal, helped to keep order, prevent looting, and aided the homeless. When the crisis was over, the Government of Bombay, usually unsympathetic to the student movement, lauded the students for their work in the difficult situation.

Other Student Activities

In 1944, a conference of medical students was convened by several noted educators. At this meeting, criticism of the medical education system and suggestions for reform were made by the students. A resolution was passed asking for the formation of a Medical Students' Union; a number of memoranda drawn up at the meeting were sent to college authorities.[8] This meeting was one of a series of meetings destined to mobilize medical students into activity and concern over their educational problems.

Other cultural groups continued to function. The Muslim Students' Union, which was trying to maintain itself as a non-political organization, sponsored lectures and debates.

[7] *Bombay Chronicle*, January 27, 1944, p. 8.
[8] Reddy, *op. cit.*, p. 217.

The Marathi Students' Association and the Youths' Parliament sponsored popular elocution competitions; such groups as the Young Men's Hindu Association and the Parsi Association had social programs in Bombay.

The All-India Students' Congress

As the nationalist student movement became more closely associated with the Indian National Congress because of their close cooperation during the independence campaigns, there was an increasing need to formally identify with the Congress. At the suggestion of the socialists within the nationalist A.I.S.F., a move was made to reorganize the student movement; the All-India Students' Congress was the result of this reorganization.[9] Three groups camp together to form the Students' Congress, the Nationalist A.I.S.F., the Forward Bloc (mainly in Bengal), and the Revolutionary Socialist Party (also centered in Bengal). The occasion for the change was the eighth session of the All-India Students' Federation which met in Bombay in January of 1945.

The tone of this first session of the Students' Congress was militant and optimistic. The influence the socialist student leaders on the meeting was clear. The speeches praised the role of the students in the 1942 struggle and urged them to become the vanguard of the political movement in India. There were few of the demoralizing factional disputes which had characterized many student meetings.[10] The only open dispute arose when many of the socialist delegates opposed the conservative Congress slogan of "one party, one programme, one leader". Since Gandhi, Sardar Patel, and other conservatives were dominating the congress the radicals felt that such a slogan would restrict them to "reactionary" policies in advance.[11]

The headquarters of the All-India Students' Congress was in Bombay, thereby allowing the student movement in Bombay to continue to exercise a strong influence on the operation of the all-India organization. Membership figures for the A.IS.C.

---

[9] *Bombay Chronicle*, January, 1, 1945, p. 2.
[10] Interview with Dalal, *loc. cit.*
[11] *Records of the All-India Students' Congress*, 1946, (in the files of Dr. A. J. Shellat, Bombay).

varied considerably. According to the Communist Journal, *The Student*, the A.I.S.C.'s membership claims ranged from 100,000 to 300,000 in early 1945, depending on the source consulted.[12]

When Maurice Dwyer, the Chancellor of the University of Delhi, expelled nationalist students, a series of demonstrations took place in various parts of India; when he visited Bombay to deliver an address at the university, he was again met by demonstrators.

The December 1946 session of the All-India Students' Congress which was held in Delhi saw the first serious factional dispute to plague the organization. The meeting was well attended, and some 1,930 delegates from all parts of India participated in the deliberations. This particular meeting was of crucial importance, for it was the first post-war meeting of the student movement, held at a time when it had become relatively certain that Indian independence was forthcoming. Thus, the student movement was at a crossroads; events were forcing it to change its tactics and much of its program.

The causes for the factional disputes and splits which have plegued the student movement since 1947 are related as much to personal rivalries as to political issues. The disturbances at the Delhi session were caused by the desire of the left-wing of the nationalist movement to assert control over the student movement. To be sure, the Communists sometimes abetted and joined disruptive elements in student meetings when this tactic suited the overall purposes of their policy. In many instances, however, particularly in the more recent period, infighting was caused by personal power conflicts and reflects only factional disagreements, not ideological conflict. Much of the talented leadership, and a substantial proportion of the rank and file members were discouraged by these trends in the internal politics of the movement and left politics altogether. The program which the students' Congress passed at its 1946 session placed more stress on campus issues. Among other things, the program of the Students' Congress included by following emphases:

1. Study classes

[12] *The Student*, August, 1946, p. 6.

2. Literacy campaigns (for Hindustani)
3. Aids to students in day to day problems
4. Village improvement work
5. Promotion of Indian culture
6. Education reform
7. Propaganda for communal harmony
8. Volunteer corps
9. Citizenship classes
10. A research center[13]

Tension was also evident between the more conservative leaders of the National Congress and the student movement. Many of the adult Congress leaders attended the A.I.S.C. meeting; Nehru, Maulana Azad, Acharaya Kripalani and others watched the proceedings intently. The students, however, seemed unwilling to bind themselves to what seemed to them to be a reactionary trend within the Congress, and a move was made to guarantee the A.I.S.C. some independence from the adult organization.

The A.I.S.C. survived the Delhi session; however, its publications were only irregularly issued and its activity fell well below its former level. The Students' Congress annually spent about Rs. 100,000. Full time volunteers worked in the national office, which remained in Bombay, and others functioned as field secretaries.[14] Repeated attempts of outside political groups to control the A.I.S.C. hampered the effectiveness of the movement. The previous working arrangement between the socialists and the Congress gradually deteriorated, and there were continuing disputes with the smaller splinter groups as well as strong opposition from the Communist dominated All-India Students' Federation. Despite these problems, however, the Students' Congress remained the largest and most active student movement in India until after independence was achieved in 1947.

At its 1946 session, the A.I.S.C. tried to transform itself from a militant arm of the independence struggle to a student orga-

---

[13] *Blitz*, January 5, 1946, p. 18.
[14] Interview with Ramkrishna Sinha, former secretary, All-India Students Congress, March 28, 1965.

nization concerned with political issues only as they related to student concerns. For many reasons, this attempt was unsuccessful. Many commentators have pointed out that the politicians then jockeying for position in the Congress were more interested in using the student movement as a tool to further their own faction than in building a viable and useful student movement. There is a good deal of truth to this allegation; pressures on the student organizations from the political groups were substantial during this period, and many of the political leaders, while urging the students to keep out of factional politics, actually pushed them into the midst of bitter disputes. The student movement itself did not seem to be ready to give up factional politics.

The 1947 session of the A.I.S.C. was held in Udaipur, the number of delegates present was smaller than in previous years. Most of the discussion was devoted to a debate of the changes which had to be made in the student movement if it was to survive. The absence of Congress leaders was symbolic of the abandonment of the student movement by the adult political organizations. The socialists had assumed control of the organizational apparatus, although they sought to accomodate as many other groups as possible. Gandhian students still participated in the organization, and the A.I.S.C. even considered cooperation with the Communist All-India Students' Federation, but when the Communist movement adopted its "militant" line late in 1947, such considerations were abandoned by both sides.

The Students' Congress realized in 1946 that the nature of the student movemen in India would have to change with the coming of independence. The 1947 session of the A.I.S.C. marked the official recognition of this fact. The movement realized that it would have to present a positive campus-based program to the students if it was to have any chance for survival.[15]

The Nationalist Student Movement in Bombay

As moves were made to reorganize the student movement, and to bring the nationalist students in closer co-operation with the

[15] Ravindra Varma, *Whither the Student Movement* (Calcutta: All-India Students' Congress, 1948), p. 40.

Congress organization, the United Committee gave way to the Bombay Students' Congress in 1945. Indeed, the Bombay Students' Congress antedated the All-India Students' Congress. Branches of the B.S.C. functioned in north and south Bombay, and in the suburbs. While the bureaucratic structure and name of the nationalist student movement in Bombay changed several times during the 1943-47 period, it continued almost without alteration. The nationalist Bombay Students' Union, the Unity Committee, and the Bombay Students' Congress were similar organizations.

In response to directives from the national organization, the B.S.C. developed an expanded the non-political setcor of its program. Several cooperative stores were set up by the student organization. The educational program of the Unity Committee and he B.S.C. continued. According to the **Bombay Chronicle**, student organizations sponsored lectures or discussion meetings at least twice a month. In 1945, a "Citizenship College" was organized by the B.S.C. . This college attracted sixty students for a month of intensive lectures and discussions on theoretical and organizational matters. The college was very successful in providing student activists with a "supplementary education" to the usual academic subjects taught in the colleges.[16]

The B.S.C. also organized an unprecedented Girl Students' convention in December of 1945. The aim of this meeting was to involve a substantial number of college girls in the activities of the student movement. Girls went into working class areas and taught leather and pottery work to the women, as well as providing literacy instruction.

When the Congress ministry took office in 1946 as a prelude to Indian independence, the students turned their attention to educational reforms and submitted a memorandum to the Minister of Education. The students stated that educational planning was necessary to assure that higher education would be available to all who wanted it. They asked that Hindustani be made the medium of instruction and that English be made a voluntary subject. Suggestions were also made for democratizing the educational system, and for improving teachers' work-

[16] *Sathi* July, 1945, p. 22.

ing conditions.[17] The memorandum was well written and thoughtful, although many of the suggestions were utopian.

Despite the interest in educational affairs, the primary focus of the movement continued to be political. The 1944 session of the Bombay Students' Conference was strongly dominated by the nationalists. Attending the meeting were 710 delegates from all of Bombay's colleges. An eleven-point program was passed, outlining the student struggle until 1947. The program made the following exhortations:

1. Fighting elements among the students should be reconciled and brought onto a common platform.
2. Honest differences are always welcome, but in spite of of their existeence, all ideologies and shades of opinion should merge in the common goal.
3. Students must prepare themselves for unbounded sacrifices.
4. The scope of students' participation in active politics during the period of their studies is very limited, and they should understand and act according to that limitation.
5. The contribution of the students to public peace can be great.
6. Students should explore the possibilities of individual civil disobedience.
7. Students can make a great contribution to the national cause by serving the Harijans (untouchables) and other groups.
8. Students can help in the agitation for the releases of the members of the Congress Working Committee.
9. The relief of people in distress due to famine, etc. should be a special task of the students.
10. Students should try to help the poor, through educational projects and other means.
11. Students should spin and wear khadi.[18]

The conference was marked by remarkable unanimity, and there were no marked changes in the direction or the leadership of

[17] *Bombay Chronicle*, August 23, 1945, p. 3.
[18] *Bombay Chronicle*, September 4, 1944, p. 1.

the student movement at that time.

In 1945, the Bombay Students' Congress was probably the largest student organization in Bombay. With 10,000 active members, the organization carried on a program in both the political and educational fields. It was a key element in the Indian National Army agitations, and some observers called it a "chhota Congress" (small Congress).[19]

When the British moved to prosecute some of the leaders of the Indian National Army (the military group which fought under Subhas Chandra Bose with the Japanese against the British), students launched a series of demonstrations to prevent prosecution from taking place. Under the leadership of the A.I.S.C. demonstrations took place in every major urban center in India. In Bombay 20,000 students went on strike and closed most of the city's colleges and schools.[20]

Many of the Students' Congress leaders, particularly the socialists, felt that they were in the vanguard of a revolution which would sweep over India upon the declaration of independence. These student leaders placed much emphasis on passing high-sounding resolutions on Indian and international issues at student conferences. The movement took an active part in several strikes of workers; it supported the teachers' struggle of 1945 and a postal strike in 1946.

As independence approached, the student movement was aware of the changing political and social climate in India. A major Bombay Students' Congress organized conference in late 1947 placed its major stress on educational and social issues. The B.S.C. sponsored an inter-school swimming contest, a boxing competition, several elocution competitions, and a parliamentary debate on "Should India join the Anglo-American bloc?" A number of cultural programs and contests also took place during this period. The B.S.C. continued its cooperative stores, and began to organize sports leagues in various colleges.

The Communist Student Movement

While the nationalist student organizations were in the forefront

---

[19] Interview with M. R. Dandavarte, Professor at Siddharth College and Chairman, Praja Socialist Party, Bombay, January 16, 1965.
[20] *The Student*, April, 1944, p. 11.

of the student movement in Bombay during the period under consideration, the Communists continued their efforts on the student level, maintaining an active organization with dedicated student cadres. The trained leadership which the Communists had built up prior to the 1942 struggle was utilized in sustaining the movement despite tremendous pressures from the nationalists.

The Communists had an organizational legitimacy which the nationalists could not discredit, for the Bombay Students' Union (Communist) and the All-India Students' Federation had functioned continuously since 1936 and had an established set of traditions. Communist student activists were encouraged to keep their scholastic records at a high level and remain on good terms with their families. The student organization took responsibility for coaching students who had fallen behind in their academic work owing to political involvement and provided informal guidance programs for students with personal or family problems. At examination time, political study circles would often turn into coaching sessions. Through these means, the Communist students were able to maintain a generally high academic record.

One of the hallmarks of the Communist movement in India at this stage was the self-sacrifice and personal integrity of its members. All these qualities engendered respect from other students; indeed, the fact that the Communst student leaders were respected personally may well have saved the movement from extinction during the height of the nationalist struggle.

The Communist student movement was, moreover, almost entirely free of communal and linguistic prejudice. Its members were in the main young people, quite "emancipated" in their social and intellectual attitudes. A fairly large proportion of dedicated young women were involved in the movement. A number of marriages grew out of the movement. Although at a severe disadvantage, Communist students were intent on facilities the war effort. They served the British government by trying to maintain domestic order and calm. In addition to propaganda campaigns stressing the importance of the fight against fascism, the B.S.U. tried to prevent student strikes. The B.S.U. even resorted to sabotage of the nationalist struggle, disrupting meetings and demonstrations. A number of observers have claimed that Communists were instrumental in leading the British authorities to key members of the underground nationalist movement, and served as a spy system for the British. An article in the Party Letter, the internal bulletin of the Communist Party, lends some weight to this charge, for it asked the students to be aware of the activities of the other nationalist student organizations, and to communicate any activities to the Communist Party office.[21]

The Communists also took an active interest in educational issues during this period, and tried to convince the student community that they were the only group interested in the welfare of the students. Both nationalists and Communists protested the results of the 1945 matriculation examination and launched campaigns against the university administration. In 1946, the B.S.U. prepared a detailed memorandum concerning proposed changes in the system of higher education. The B.S.U. memorandum stated that the need for more colleges in Bombay was great, and pointed out that only thirty colleges existing in Bombay Presidency and that seven were opened between 1939 and 1946. In 1939, the student body was 15,320, and by 1944 it had increased to 22,149. In Bombay city, there were 7,805 college students in 1944, or one-third of the total number in the entire province. Detailed demands for increased hostels and library facilities were also presented in this document.[22]

In addition to their concern with educational issues, the B.S.U. was particularly interested in Hindu-Muslim unity. The B.S.U. celebrated such holidays as Iqbal Day. When a proposal was made for talks between the Muslim League and the Congress, the Communist students were strongly in favor of this and were generally sympathetic to the Muslim demand for an independent Pakistan. The Communists were on better terms with the communal minded Muslims than with the nationalist movement.

The B.S.U. was comparatively large during this period, although the organization lost a good deal of its membership

---

[21] *Party Letter*, February 19, 1943, p. 8.

[22] Bombay Students' Union, *Memorandum to the Minister of Education on College Education in Bombay* (Bombay: Bombay Students' Union, 1946), p. 3.

after 1942. According to *The Student*, whose estimate is probably high, the B.S.U. had a membership of 5,000 in the Bombay Presidency, (compared to 50,000 in Bengal).[23] The A.I.S.F. publication, edited and published from Bombay, claimed a circulation of 13,000 and was issued monthly.

The activities of the Communist student organizations followed closely the changes and developments in the Communist Party itself. Indeed, during the 1943-45 period, there was little question that the B.S.U. was a direct appendage of the Communist Party, so closely was it allied with the Party's work. By 1946, strong attempts were being made to rebuild the weakened organization, and a more militant policy was undertaken by the Communist movement in India. Indeed, the Congress was being attacked as reactionary, and the stage was being set for the "revolutionary" period which started in 1948. The Communist student movement, because of its growing militancy, was able to recoup some of its losses, although the movement never regained the importance it had achieved in the late 1930's.

The fact that the Communist student movement was able to keep the loyalty of such a substantial proportion of its membership during this period is quite significant, and indicates the attraction of the Communist ideology to the student community. Even though the Communists were opposed to the main trends in Indian political life at the time, and had virtually no independent existence outside the directives of the Party, they continued to be a force among the students of Bombay. The relative success of the Communist movement among the students in the face of substantial odds is partially understandable in view of its trained core of committed and able leadership and ability to retain the loyalty of these ideologically oriented students.

The Student Movement as a "Vanguard of Revolution": The Naval Mutiny of 1946

Most of the discussion in this chapter has been concerned with the role of the political student movement in the nationalist movement and the political life of Bombay and of India during

---
[23] *The Student*, October, 1943, p. 24.

this period. On several occasions, the student movement played a significant role in the broader mass movement sweeping across the subcontinent. One of these occasions was the mutiny of the Royal Indian Navy which started in Bombay, and later spread to other cities in 1946. Although the mutiny was not initiated by the students, and the student movement did not make it a success, the role of the students was important, and the events of that important week in 1946 had some important implications for the student leadership and movement in Bombay.

In mid-February 1946, when the sailors of the Royal Indian Navy based at Bombay disobeyed their British officers and for a short period threatened to precipitate a massive revolutionary struggle, the city of Bombay entered one of the most critical periods in almost two decades of nationalist agitation. The causes for the mutiny were related not so much to broader political issues as to conditions within the navy. But when the mutiny had started, it took on nationalist overtones, and spread to other elements of the city's population. Within a matter of two or three days, sections of the working class had joined the sailors and much of Bombay was under the control of rebellious elements. Students provided support in the form of demonstrations.

The mutiny stimulated the students to envision a social revolution which might oust the British from the subcontinent and simultaneously bring social change to India. The leftist leaders of the student movement, both nationalist and Communist, felt that the mutiny might be the spark of such a revolution, and they therefore stressed its importance. Student leaders seriously discussed the possibility of more widespread outbreaks. Political leaders, who attempted to expand the mutiny from a military rebellion with limited goals to a broader outbreak, succeeded in giving the mutiny a nationalist political flavor.

After four days of agitation, however, British forces succeeded in quelling the disturbances. A high level mission from the Congress Working Committee in New Delhi came to Bombay and tried to arrange a settlement of the mutiny without further bloodshed. The Congress leadership, particularly the conservatives within the organization's inner circle, were anxious that the mutiny be settled quickly. At this time the Congress was on the verge of signing an agreement with the British authorities for a peaceful transfer of power and the creation of an independent India, and many Congressmen did not wish to jeopardize the negotiations at such an important juncture. Conservative Congressmen were genuinely afraid of a social revolution, and had both financial and political reasons for wishing the creation of an independent Indian state without a revolutionary upheaval.

A settlement was reached, and the mutineers virtually capitulated. The students and other radical leaders of the mutiny in Bombay felt as if the revolution had been betrayed; they were particularly vehement against the Congress leadership, who, they felt, had unnecessarily compromised an important struggle. The Congress leadership continued its negotiations for independence in New Delhi, and the rest of the country bided its time until the announcement of British withdrawal was made. The mutiny probably hastened British withdrawal, for it helped convince them that the mainstay of their power on the subcontinent, the armed forces, was unreliable.

The naval mutiny can be seen as the beginning of the end for the militant political student movement in Bombay. For the first time, the student leaders felt that they had been betrayed not by the British, but by their own adult leaders. Congress officials did not consult the students during their negotiations with the British; after the mutiny, statesmen and politicians did not seem to regard students as an important element in the political equation in India.[34]

Conclusion

Most of the important elements that led to the decline of the student movement in Bombay can be seen in this period. While the student movement continued to play an active if less important role in the nationalist movement, there were indications that changes were taking place both on the campus and in society. It is an unwritten law of social movements that

[34] For a more detailed discussion of the Bombay Naval Mutiny, see Philip G. Altbach, "The Bombay Naval Mutiny", *Opinion*, VI, No. 12, July 27, 1965, pp. 40-45.

perods of intensive struggle cannot be sustained indefinitely, and the almost inevitable loss of momentum after the 1942 effort took place between late 1943 and 1946. Furthermore, the nationalist movement itself became less struggle-oriented as World War II ended and British authorities became more amenable to Indian self-government.

The influence of left-wing ideas was strong among students and, in their minds, social revolution was a prerequisite for national independence. Furthermore, many students participated in the nationalist campaigns not out of ideological commitment but for the excitement surrounding such ventures. When the militancy of the movement was dissipated and participants were no longer asked to join demonstrations but were told to raise the literacy rate or discuss constitutional problems, many students lost interest in the movement altogether.

The student leadership did not change its orientation to meet the new reality of Indian political life. While the student movement remained interested in agitational issues, the Congress was preparing to constitutionally assume power. Although socialism was one of the stated goals of the Congress leadership, India was far from a socialist state, and many of those with substantial power in the Congress were quite conservative in their political views. Furthermore, while the students remained ready to participate in mass demonstrations, their own leaders in the Congress organization were urging them to return to their classes and leave politics to the politicians. Student leaders felt that this was a betrayal and that no recognition was being given to their role in the independence movement. Educational issues became more pressing as enrolment expanded rapidly. Yet the leadership of the student movement took almost no interest in educational problems.

As a result of these changes, and the fact that the student organizations were unwilling to undergo transformations to meet a radically different situation, most of the members of the various student groups, particularly the nationalist organizations, left the student movement altogether and became politically inactive. The leadership became frustrated by its inability to arouse support among the students. The naval mutiny and other events convinced the student leaders that compromise with the *status quo* leadership of the Congress meant destruction of their revolutionary goals, and disillusionment of both leaders and rank and file resulted.

CHAPTER VII

STUDENTS AND POLITICS SINCE 1947

INDEPENDENT INDIA came into being with relative ease, although the trauma of partition and the communal disturbances which accompanied it put the fledgling government to the test within days of its assumption of office. Many of the changes took place in India during this period had important implications for the student movement. The transformation of the Congress from a mass movement into a pragmatic political machine disillusioned many of the more idealistic of the student leaders. Student organizations had done little to prepare themselves for independence; in spite of a renewed interest in campus issues, the agitational approach remained the hallmark of the movement. The refusal of the students to follow the lead of the Congress in making a transformation to "normalcy" caused the dramatic break between the adult leaders of the Congress and the student movement. While Nehru and the other Congress leaders had given unqualified support to the students during the independence struggle, their attitude changed drastically and abruptly following independence.

The Response of the Student Movement to Change in Society

The student movement does not function in a vacuum. It is sensitive to changes in the educational system and the nation's political and social climate. The Indian student movement, in particular, has been a creature of its environment. The foregoing discussion has shown that the major motivation of the student movement during the 1943-1947 period was the political situation, specifically, the nationalist struggle which occupied the center of the political stage. The educational system in Bombay was expanding at a rapid rate. Enrolments continued to grow during this period and the student population grew by almost one-third in Bombay city. Most of the increase took place in the newer institutions, while the older colleges remained relatively stable. Several new colleges were established in the suburbs and a larger number of midddle class students were able to attend institutions of higher education.

The government had already begun to spend substantial sums of money on the technical institutions, with a decreased emphasis on the liberal arts colleges. The problems of these technical schools and colleges, many of which were set up hastily and lacking traditions on which to base themselves, were immediately evident to the students. Strikes took place at these technical schools during this period, indicating the ambivalent attitude which existed.

The traditional pattern of a liberal arts education for a select few was in disrepute, as the society grew more complex and demanded more skilled manpower to operate and repair the machines. The area of the gentleman-administrator was at an end. Funds for the expansion of educational institutions were limited, and no central planning was undertaken by the various governmental agencies involved with education. Expansion took place, but it was done according to local initiative and was often both haphazard and lacking in adequate standards. The central government had assumed a laissez-faire attitude toward education.

The reaction of the student movement to these changes which were taking place in Bombay was notably apathetic. Most of the student organizations were so immersed in the political struggle that their involvement with educational problems was superficial; when student proposals for reforms were presented, they were often made in the interest of politics rather than in the interest of the educational system. The Communist student movement, for its part, was hampered by its dogmatic assumptions about the nature of education and society; nevertheless, statements on education by the Communist student organizations during this period showed more insight and foresight than those of the nationalists. Other student groups took only a marginal interest in these issues. Typically, the student movement reacted to the state of affairs only when a specific situation became intolerable.

The problem of shifting the emphasis of the student movement is based not only in the overtly political organizations but in attitudes of both teachers and students in India. Educational authorities did not encourage students to examine critically or constructively the basis of the educational system. These memoranda and recommendations, many quite reasonable, which were submitted to educators and to government officials responsible for education, fell on deaf ears for the most part. Observers of Indian higher education have pointed out that the educational system itself is quite rigid and does not encourage or prepare for independent thinking or action by the students. The all important examination system is administered by outside authorities, and normally no recourse is possible except through non-constitutional methods such as agitation or strike. Furthermore, there is little contact between teacher and student in the Indian college, thereby leaving the student with even less feeling of identification with the institution. Cut off from almost all channels of communication with the educational authorities, the students fell into apathy or turned to what has become known as "indiscipline".

The Youth Congress in a Changing Student Movement

The Bombay Student's Congress continued to function after 1947. Its leadership attempted to substitute political involvement by cultural and social service activities. A seminar on economics was organized in 1947, and a contest to select the "best built collegian" was held in the same year. Seminars and beauty contests are a sharp contrast to the sabotage work of only a few years before. One of the few processions which the B.S.C. sponsored in 1948 was in homage to Gandhi.

During this period, the B.S.C. was beset by severe organizational and financial problems. Without financial support from the adult political parties, the students found it very difficult to maintain their office headquarters. Obtaining a quorum for executive meetings of the B.S.C. became a challenge. However, the fact that there were meetings of the B.S.C. secretaries at the various colleges in Bombay during the 1950's indicated that the organization was at least functioning on a minimal scale.[1]

By late 1948, it became clear that the Students' Congress could not survive. The socialists who had been responsible

---

[1] Interview with Prabhakar Kunte, Secretary, Transport Workers' Union, Bombay; former Secretary, Bombay Students' Union, January 10, 1965.

for much of the B.S.C. leadership in earlier periods and still exercised more than a little influence over the organization, were then in a process of reorganizing their own youth program and placed much less emphasis on student work.

In India, the distinction between youth and student organizations is difficult to make, since most non-student youths have neither the sophistication nor the time to participate to any substantial degree in voluntary organizations. In such groups as the Youth Congress, students or former students are invariably in leadership positions, and constitute a substantial proportion of the membership. It is also difficult to communicate with non-student young people in India, since they seldom constitute a definable group. It is much easier to contact students, who congregate on college campuses.

The unclear relationship between youth and student organizations is reflected in the transition from the All-India Students' Congress to the Youth Congress indicated the desire of the Congress leadership to remain an active force among young people. As the group become more bureaucratized, many students lost interest. While the organizational ties between the Students' Congress of the pre-Independence period and the Youth Congress of the post-1947 period are not direct, both groups represent efforts of the Congress to organize on the youth level.

In Bombay, the first Youth Congress organization was established in 1949 at the initiative of the Bombay Provincial Congress Committee (B.P.C.C.). The Youth Congress was administered by an executive committee, under the strong influence of the B.P.C.C. and thereby subservient to the adult Congress organization. The executive committee included representatives from the ward Youth Congress affiliates and from the B.P.C.C. itself. In a short time, the Youth Congress was able to attract about 12,000 members, with nearly 1,000 active workers.[2] Although substantial proportion of these members were not students and probably not eevn youths, a number did come from colleges. The Youth Congress tried to attract students, organizing several debates and a mock parliament for the benefit of the student community.

[2] Interview with R. Rajda, former Secretary, Bombay Pradesh Youth Congress, March 3, 1965.

The working committee of the All-India Congress Committee, the highest policy-making body of the Congress, noted with satisfaction the development of the Youth Congress and proposed a constitution for the organization. Among the objectives of the constitution were the following:

1. to promote development of character and discipline;
2. to organize study circles and classes;
3. to help with constructive work in cooperation with the National Congress;
4. to promote sports;
5. to assist the Congress in combating communalism;
6. to work in rural areas.[3]

It is significant that there is no mention of an educational or political function of the Youth Congress. In the early period the Youth Congress offered guidance services to students, and because of its close connections with political leaders, the organization was often able to secure admission to a college for students and advise them on courses of study and related matters.

The idealism of the independence struggle was almost eliminated, and opportunism became a part of everyday life in Indian politics. In Bombay, the problem of ambitious politicians was compunded by serious ethnic divisions within the Congress. The Bombay Provincial Congress Committee was dominated by Bombay's Gujarati minority during the period after Independence; the Youth Congress was also controlled by this group to the almost total exclusion of the Maharashtrians.[4] Disputes between the "ruling" groups in the Bombay Congress, which were on the whole conservative, and those Congressmen who favored a more radical social program also had their effect on the Youth Congress. As the Youth Congress became a recognized part of the Congress machinery, many young politicians tried to obtain leadership in the organization with the intention of using it as a springboard to higher offices.

One of the reasons for the lack of mass support for the

[3] *Bombay Chronicle*, October 21, 1949, p. 6.
[4] Interview with Adam Adil, Secretary of the Bombay Congress, March 11, 1965.

Youth Congress prior to 1958 may have been the fact that the organization did not have democratic procedures to govern its functioning. According to several observers, a small clique was able to effectively control the organization by manipulation of the working committee. Although the "paper" membership of the Bombay Youth Congress was 10,000 in 1958 and the Bombay branch sent 125 delegates to the All-India convention of the Youth Congress, it is doubtful whether the organization played any significant role among the students or the youth of Bombay.[5] As the Youth Congress developed and became a stable organization in Bombay, its level of activity fell even lower. By 1958, it was estimated that the group had only 200 active members, whose commitment consisted of little more than regular attendance at meetings.

The Communist Student Movement in Bombay

It is easier to examine the Communist student movement in the past thirty years than any of the other organizations, for this segment of the student movement has maintained a clear organizational structure since the formation of the All-India Students' Federation in 1936.

While the Communists have never dominated the student community, they have exercised a consistent and often substantial influence on it. The Communist Party, unlike most of its rivals, has retained an interest in the student movement, and has devoted both time and energy to its student fronts. Like the rest of the movement, the Communist organizations, notably the All-India Students' Federation and its affiliate the Bombay Students' Union, have lost much of their strength and appeal since 1947.

One factor which distinguishes the Communist student organizations from most other student groups in India is the dependence of the students on the policies and directives of the Communist Party. Previous discussions have shown that the Communist student movement has jeopardized itself on several occasions because of its strong support of unpopular

[5] Interview with M. Sethna, Chairman, Post-Graduate Students' Union, University of Bombay, March 11, 1965.

stands of the Communist Party. The most graphic example of this was the 1942 movement, which was strongly opposed by the Communists, despite the almost unanimous support for the struggle from the student community.

By 1947, the membership of the B.S.U. had reached its peak, with more than 10,000 supporters. B.S.U. units were functioning in most of Bombay's colleges, night schools, and many secondary schools. It sponsored a "Demands Day" and asked that the students boycott their classes in support of demands for educational reforms and lowered college fees. The B.S.U. also strongly supported the idea of student unity, and seemed to be sincerely in cooperation with other student groups.

The Bombay Students' Union sponsored a number of activities which showed a good deal of imagination and initiative. In an attempt to organize the growing number of students attending night schools, the B.S.U. organized a convention of night school students and attracted representatives of 15,000 students. The B.S.U. also supported the demands of the teachers' union for higher wages. A leaflet outlining the program of the B.S.U. stressed primarily student demands and problems. It also demanded that India withdraw from the British Commonwealth. On several occasions, the B.S.U. worked through an ad hoc front group, called the City Students' Action Committee, to achieve its aims. This means was devised to obtain a wider support than the B.S.U. itself could attract, and usually succeeded in this task.

A change in the policy of the international Communist movement in late 1947 caused a drastic alteration in the policy of the Communist Party of India, as well as in its student fronts. When Stalin was convinced that the world situation was ripe for the rapid advance of Communism after the Second World War, he ordered Communist movements in the areas not under his direct control to obtain governmental power by any means. This drastic change from mild "united front" of cooperation with non-Communist movements and governments which had been in effect during the war to a militant "hard" line caused severe strains in the Indian Communist movement.

The Communist student movement was very much involved in the "adventurist" revolutionary policy of the Communist Party, for its emphasis on sabotage and exiciting political struggle had a strong appeal among the militant workers of the All-India Students' Federation. For the rank and file supporters, this new policy proved too militant, and a large proportion of the "fellow travelers" and many less committed A.I.S.F. members left during this period. The strength of the Communists in various student unions, for example, declined seriously.[6]

One of the most important events in Bombay during this period was 1947 annual session of the All-India Students' Federation. Coming at the beginning of the "adventurist" period, it was an indication of Communist activity at this time. The Government of Bombay, fearing communal violence, had banned all public meetings and had cancelled special permission for the A.I.S.F. meeting only a few days before it was to begin, after many of the delegates had already arrived from outside Bombay.[7]

The executive committee of the A.I.S.F. decided to defy the ban, and attempts were made to begin the meeting as scheduled. A procession of 2,500 students was stopped by the police; in the skirmish, the police fired on the students, injuring three.[8] The aims of the A.I.S.F. were achieved by this meeting, which not only communicated the new revolutionary policy of the organization to the 3,000 delegates, but gave the students an example of the agitational approach which was to mark the Communist student movement during the following several years.

In 1948, the B.S.U. could count on about fifty activities, most of whom were also members of the Communist Party. Meetings sponsored by the B.S.U. were well attended. The Communist leadership realized the potential usefulness of students to the Communist movement. A number of observers have said that the Party used the students as cannon fodder for the movement, and it is true that a large number of students were jailed during this period, some for up to two years. While other segments of the Party had reservations about the advisability

---

[6] Interview with Vaman Poonja, Secretary, Blitz National Forum, former Secretary, Bombay Students' Union, March 12, 1965.

[7] *Bombay Chronicle*, December 29, 1947, p. 6.

[8] *Bombay Chronicle*, January 1, 1948, p. 1.

of the revolutionary struggle, the students remained firmly committed to the militant line.

When the militant leadership in the Communist Party collapsed and the Party reverted back to its more traditional student emphasis on campus issues and on constructive work, the Communist student movement had almost been destroyed. Many of the students who had sacrificed themselves during the "adventurist" period quit the student movement. Some students suffered substantially during this period—some were disowned by their families, others underwent long jail sentences, and still others were forced to end their college careers. It is understandable that the abrupt and unsuccessful end to a long struggle caused much disillusionment among these cadres.

By the mid-Fifties, the emphasis of the B.S.U. had shifted almost entirely to social and cultural affairs, and the agitational approach of previous periods had almost disappeared. Its identity as a Communist-dominated group was de-emphasized, and the study circles which had been so effective in indoctrinating young people were virtually discontinued.[9] During this period, the B.S.U. sponsored annual debating competitions, cultural shows, and similar activities.

Although it was able to maintain its offices during the entire post-war period (probably with the financial assistance of the Communist Party), the B.S.U. had deteriorated seriously by 1959, and an attempt was made in that year to reorganize the group in order to permit its expansion to the campuses in Bombay. An "inaugural meeting" was held, a constitution passed, and some plans were made for future activities. The B.S.U. grew somewhat during the 1958-60 academic year, although it did not succeed in re-establishing itself as a major student organization. The membership of the B.S.U. fell below 1,000, and only a handful were actively involved in the day to day operation of the group. The few agitational issues which the organization did take up during this period, such as the morning college question, were primarily concerned with working class students. The ineffectiveness of the B.S.U. is indicated by its failure to launch a successful agitation against a fee increase imposed by the university. Current B.S.U. mem-

[9] Interview with Poonja,. *loc. cit.*

bers are not very interested in politics, and the B.S.U. leaders, many of whom are still Communists, have not placed great emphasis on recruiting Party members from the student movement. The present membership of the Bombay Students' Union is approximately 2,000, although only a small proportion of this number is active in the organization.[10]

The formation of leadership and exercise of power is as crucial in the Indian Communist student movement as it is in any Communist movement. During the period when the movement was an important political factor in Bombay, and particularly during the Ranadive period, the Party exercised strict control over the local groups of the B.S.U. Each college cell of the B.S.U. had at least one member of the Communist Party who provided direction to the local group. These Communist cadres within the B.S.U. met periodically with adult Party leaders to discuss organizational plans and work out ideological questions. By a high level of political sophistication and careful organization, a relatively small minority of Communists in the B.S.U. was able to effectively control the organization. The power in the B.S.U. office rested not so much with the general secretary, but with a committee of four or five politically matured students who had selected him and who worked closely with him.[11]

It was estimated that there were only fifty or sixty Communist Party members in the B.S.U. in 1949, when the organization had a total membership of almost 20,000. Yet it was possible for the Communists to effectively control the organization.

The development of the Communist student movement in Bombay did not differ radically from the rest of the student movement. Perhaps a substantial blame for the decline of the movement can be traced to the organizational and political blunders of the Communist Party itself, rather than to outside circumstances. Since 1953, the Communist student movement has been unable to rebuild its strength or to infuse any political meaning into the movement which has remained. In this, it is not different from the other student political organizations in Bombay.

[10] Interview with P. Redkar, Secretary, Bombay Teachers' Union, March 19, 1965.
[11] Interview with Poonja, *loc. cit.*

The Socialist Student Movement

Indian socialism has a long, if somewhat chequered, history. The first organized democratic socialist movement on an all-India basis was the Congress Socialist Party, which was formed in 1934 by a group of socialists within the Congress. Indian socialism has been influenced much more by the pragmatism of British leftists than by Marx or, more recently, by Russian thinking.

The socialists were one of the first groups to take an interest in the student community. In Bombay, particularly, the early socialists were also influential on the thinking and actions of the student movement. Socialists like S. M. Joshi and particularly Yusuf Meherally were pioneers of the student movement in Maharashtra and Bombay. During most of the independence struggle, the socialist leaders provided guidance for the nationalist student movement. Many of the socialist intellectuals of the present period were recruited from the student movement, probably a higher proportion than any of the other political groups in India, with the possible exception of the Communists.

Prior to Independence, the socialists had never had a separate student organization. While the Communists were well organized in the All-India Students' Federation, the socialists were but one of many factions within the nationalist student movement. When the Congress Socialists split from the Congress in 1948, the lack of a student affiliate was felt by the party leaders; and a move was made to form a student wing of the Socialist Party.[12]

After Independence, the dominant trend in socialist thinking on the student movement was to support broader and more representative student organizations, rather than to found another group. The socialists strongly supported the formation of the National Union of Students in 1950. Jayaprakash Narayan, a leading socialist at this time and probably the most popular leader among the students, gave the keynote address at the inaugural conference of the National Union of Students.

[12] *Bombay Chronicle*, October 12, 1948, p. 10.

Many of the socialist leaders realized by 1953 that a mass student movement in India was no longer a possibility in the light of educational and political developments. Steps were taken to build an organization which could provide the basis of young leadership for the Socialist Party and disseminate socialist ideas to the student community. In 1950, a socialist student study camp was held in Bombay; on the program were intensive ideological discussions and speeches by Ashoka Mehta and other socialist leaders.[13] Later in the 1950s, socialist students were active in the various colleges "mock parliaments" held regularly around the year in Bombay. Through these programs socialist ideas were brought to the student community.

In 1953, the Samajwadi Yuvak Sabha (Socialist Youth Organization) was formed on national basis, a branch also being formed in Bombay at this time. The national office of the S.Y.S. was in Bombay. In 1953, the Samajwadi Yuvak Sabha had about 1,500 members in Bombay, a large proportion of whom were students. The S.Y.S. claimed effective representation from twelve of Bombay's twenty-eight colleges at this time, in addition to a group of post-graduate students who held regular meetings.[14] No attempt was made to impose an ideological position on the study circles, although a general socialist approach was emphasized. The topics of discussion concerned current economic and political events and more cultural subjects as well.

Although the main emphasis of the socialist student movement was on educational activity, it took some interest in agitational issues. In 1950, for example, a Students' Action Committee was formed in Bombay under the leadership of the socialists which was successful in preventing a proposed increase in college fees from taking place.[15] During the early 1950s the socialists sponsored a regular study class for students which attracted thirty or forty students each week. Owing to a lack of key leadership, this program did not last more than

[13] *Bombay Chronicle*, September 25, 1950, p. 8.
[14] Interview with Vijay Pradhan, Secretary, Samajwadi Yuvak Sabha, Bombay, March 1, 1965.
[15] Interview with Ahmad Zakaria, former secretary of the Bombay Youth Congress, March 3, 1965.

a few years.[16]

One of the few agitational efforts in which the S.Y.S. engaged took place in 1955, when the socialist movement was stressing a satayagraha campaign against the Portugese government in Goa. Socialist students were able to launch a strike which closed most of Bombay's colleges for a day. Students were a key element in the agitation, which involved thousands of workers in Bombay and received widespread attention.

In 1957, the S.Y.S. agitated for the retention of English at the secondary school level in Maharashtra, stating that an adequate knowledge of English was necessary for college education in the present system.[17] The S.Y.S. has been one of the few student organizations which has consistently supported English, stressing the importance of maintaining the quality of education. This particular effort was unsuccessful in that only a small number of students were interested in this issue.

Since 1959, the activity of the S.Y.S. has declined. Today, only a handful of students in Bombay have even heard of the organization. No study circles have functioned on a continuous basis since 1959; all other activity has been sporadic. The S.Y.S. had about 500 members in Bombay in 1963, although this figure is probably somewhat exaggerated. One observer has said that perhaps twenty young people are involved actively in S.Y.S. work, mostly young professionals or post-graduate students; there is no full-time staff working for the organization.[18]

The Samajwadi Yuvak Sabha has not been the only socialist student organization to function in Bombay in recent years. The Rashtra Seva Dal, a socialist sponsored youth movement, has been an interesting experiment with a different kind of student organization in India. Although not limited to students, the R.S.D. has involved large numbers of students in its activities.

The Rashtra Seva Dal tried to involve young people in a "total" program. The emphasis was not distinctly political, nor was agitational activity a part of the R.S.D.'s approach. Rather, the emphasis was placed on social service, and on a

[16] Interview with Dr. Usha Mehta, *loc cit.*
[17] Interview with Pradhan, *loc. cit.*
[18] *Ibid.*

character building program of athletics, study, and constructive work. In the beginning, the R.S.D. was organized along neighbourhood lines, or in the smaller towns of Maharashtra, and built up strong groups. The leadership of the movement was openly socialist, and many R.S.D. members participated in socialist activity such as agitational campaigns before Independence and later in election campaigns.

Between 1943 and 1950, the Rashtra Seva Dal was a powerful force in Maharashtra, exercising a strong influence on the cultural and social life of the state, particularly in the medium sized towns. There were two university chapters of the R.S.D., both in Bombay, involving about 150 students from various colleges in the city. In addition to these groups, the R.S.D. had more than 4,000 members among high school students.[19] The R.S.D. sponsored coaching classes for the S.S.C. examinations and weekly discussion groups for the students in addition to its regular program of physical exercise and games. Many students were involved in the cultural activities of the organization, and summer camps were sponsored which involved students in constructive work in the villages. While the R.S.D. did not engage in political agitation at any time, it did add to the political education of its members, giving them both an ideological education and organizational training.

During the communal tension following Independence, the R.S.D. organized defence squads to prevent communal violence. The organization was widely recognized for its service during this period. The R.S.D. took a strong position against caste and communal affiliations and strongly supported inter-caste marriages. The fact that more than 100 inter-caste marriages took place among R.S.D. activity during the 1950s lent weight to the effectiveness of its propaganda.[20]

By the late 1950s, the mass appeal of the R.S.D. seemed to have ended, and the organization did not exercise the influence which it had previously exerted. Its membership remained at 10,000 in Maharashtra and about 1,100 in Bombay, but its leadership was no longer as committed as it was before the

[19] Interview with S. S. Varde, professor at National College, Bandra, February 20, 1965.
[20] Interview with Nana Dengle, Secretary, Rashtra Seva Dal, January 2, 1965.

decline of the organization.[21] The college R.S.D. groups no longer exist. Its impact on the student community, which was never great, has become almost negligible in recent years. R.S.D. officials have said that they are unable to concentrate on college students due to limited staff and facilities.

The Right-Wing Student Movement

The right-wing political movement in India is somewhat more difficult to understand than the leftist movement, since its roots lie for the most part in Hindu tradition rather than in Western secular ideology. In the early part of this century, men like Swami Vivekananda and Tilak were calling on the Indian people to return to Hinduism in order to regain their self-respect. This Hindu revival was linked to nationalism and to traditional social customs. Such reforms as the outlawing of *sati* (immolation of widows), campaigns against the dowry system, etc. often met with opposition from revivalist elements. These groups often placed a major portion of the blame for India's decline on the various "alien" groups which had settled in the country. Muslims, Christians, and others were looked down upon, and it was claimed that Hinduism and Indian nationalism were necessarily related.

At the time when the Congress was expanding from a small, middle class reformist organization to a mass movement, another group was formed in the heartland of Hindu nationalism. The Rashtriya Swayamsevak Sangh (R.S.S.) was organized in Nagpur in 1925. The original purpose of the R.S.S. was not political, and to this day the organization avoids partizan politics. The R.S.S. was founded to work for the moral and cultural revival of the Hindu nation. It advocates a "militant awareness of their (Hindu) common heritage and destiny."[22] While recognizing that the British should leave the government of India to the Hindus, the main attacks of the R.S.S. were against the Muslims who were felt to be the alien invaders. One of the early motives of the R.S.S. in its early

---

[21] Rashtra Seva Dal, *Annual Report, 1963* (Bombay: Rashtra Seva Dal, 1963), p. 5.

[22] J. A. Curran, Jr., *Militant Hnduism in Indian Politics: A Study of the R.S.S.* (New York: Institute for Pacific Relations, 1951), p. 5.

days was Maharashtrian nationalism; the organization has always been strong in Maharashtra and particularly among the high-caste Brahmins. The R.S.S. remained a small organization of about 500 members until about 1932, and did not extend beyond Maharashtra until 1937. The launching of Ghandhi's non-Cooperation Movement in 1930 marked a low point for the R.S.S., and many of its members joined in the Congress struggle. By 1938, however, the organization grew to about 40,000 members in most parts of India but with heavy concentration in the Hindi speaking areas of north India.[23]

By 1950, the R.S.S. had grown to substantial proportions, with close to 500,000 members in Bombay state, most of them in Maharashtra. In 1949, the R.S.S. launched a series of protests against the imprisonment of its key leaders, and some 50,000 people were arrested. It is clear that the R.S.S. constitutes a semi-political movement in India with important mass strength. Its ideological approach has been somewhat modified since 1948 to de-emphasize its extreme communalism, although the organization continues to frighten India's Muslim minority and is strongly opposed by people who favor a secular form of government for India. The size of the R.S.S. membership is somewhat offset by the fact that its appeal is limited to certain social classes and castes within the society. It has been mentioned that a large proportion of the membership is Brahmin, although the R.S.S. is not popular at the "elite" colleges and draws most of the its support from lower middle class students. Furthermore, it has very little support in the non-Hindi-speaking areas, and naturally does not attract members of minority communities.[24]

The idoelogy of the R.S.S. has a strong attraction for the more conservative elements of Hindu society. It has a relatively simple appeal for a return to the original Hindu virtues of honesty, strength, and truth. The R.S.S. strongly advocates Hindi as the Indian national language, and there is much antipathy to English and Western values. The Vedas and other Hindu religious classics are seen as the highest achivement of mankind. R.S.S. intellectuals point out that the airplane,

[23] *Ibid.*, p. 15.
[24] Interview with M. Gokhale, Assistant Editor, *Maharashtra Times*, former activist in the R.S.S., February 10, 1965.

among other things, was foreseen in the Vedas, and that the Hindu religious classics hold the answers to all of mankind's problems. The R.S.S. holds that India is a Hindu nation and that Hindus should govern it. The organization is unclear about the status of the minority religions within a "Hindu" India, although they do state that "unpatriotic elements" should be eliminated.[25]

The strongest appeal of the R.S.S. has been to high school students. The bulk of recruits come from this age group and little recruiting is done in the colleges. The program of the R.S.S. is often too elementary for college students, although many college students who have belonged to the R.S.S. before entering college continue to remain active in the organization. While the left-wing student organizations have attracted some of the most intelligent students in the colleges, the R.S.S. has recruited a broad range of students.[26] Despite this fact, the R.S.S. had about 5,000 college members by 1950 who participated in regular neighbourhood R.S.S. groups. Even the Communist student journal recognized that the R.S.S. had a strong base among college and high school students in Maharashtra.[27]

The appeal of the R.S.S. among college students has, however, declined in recent years. Like the other student organizations, the R.S.S. has been a victim of the general apathy which pervades many campuses in India. Furthermore, communalism is not "respectable" in cities like Bombay.

If the R.S.S. has lost most of its attraction among students, another right-wing student organization has grown up to take its place. The Akhil Bharatiya Vidyarthi Parishad (All India Students' Organization), is a direct descendent of the R.S.S. The Vidyarthi Parishad was formed in an attempt to make the Hindu nationalist movement relevant to the present day student community; to date this attempt has proved quite successful in Bombay. Like the R.S.S., the Vidyarthi Parishad claims to be a non-political organization which has traditionally steered away from participation in partizan politics. It has also eschewed demonstrations and agitational activity as much as

[25] Interview with D. Laud, R.S.S. activist, January 24, 1965.
[26] Interview with Laud, *loc. cit.*
[27] *The Student*, July, 1942, p. 20.

possible and has tried to work in cooperation with school administrators.

Despite its non-political protestations, the Vidyarthi Parishad is clearly political in its ideology and a number of right-wing political leaders have acknowledged their debt to this relatively new student organization. The organization has avoided directly political issues, although it has engaged in several fairly successful agitations against increases in university fees. A leader of the Jan Sangh stated that many active party workers are recruited from the Vidyarthi Parishad, and that the Jan Sangh uses the Parishad as a training ground for its future activists.[28]

The Vidyarthi Parishad was founded in Bombay in 1955 by a number of former R.S.S. students who felt that a more sophisticated approach to student organization was necessary. It had a nucleus of members at four Bombay colleges and succeeded in attracting 200 students fairly quickly.[29] From the beginning, the Vidyarthi Parishad stressed the importance of the students' organizing themselves for their own welfare.

The Vidyarthi Parishad claims 10,000 members in Bombay. Although this membership figure is undoubtably exaggerated, it is probably true that the Parishad has the largest number of members of any student organization in Bombay. In addition, it claims 150 active student workers, a figure which is probably close to the truth.[30] With this number of active supporters, the Parishad has an important advantage over its rivals in Bombay.

Ideologically, the Vidyarthi Parishad is an intellectual's R.S.S., but its approach is moderate enough not to drive away prospective members. It does not stress its communalist background, and claims to be a non-communal group. It is strongly nationalist and anti-Communist, but does not take stands for or against any political parties (except the Communists). It has not openly attacked the Muslims, although in private conversation many members will cast doubts on the patriotism of Indian Muslims. The organization takes pride in celebrating

---

[28] Interview with Pandit, *loc. cit.*
[29] Interview with Pandit, *loc cit.*
[30] Interview with P. B. Acharya, Secretary, Akhil Bharatiya Vidyarthi Parishad, February 22, 1965.

the birthdays of such leaders as Swami Vivekananda, Tilak, and other Hindu nationalists. The organization is strongly opposed to what are called "anti-national" elements, and defines these in its own terms.

The Vidyarthi Parishad has strongly emphasized the partnership between the students, the college professors and administration, trying, without much success, to involve professors in its work. Although most teachers and administrators consider the group to be a right-wing communalist front and have steered clear of it, they admit that the Parishad has done valuable work while avoiding the agitational path so typical of student groups in India. The Vidyarthi Parishad considers the teacher a "father" to his students; the organization advises that conflicts between teachers and students be avoided.[31]

At the 1964 annual convention of the Vidyarthi Parishad, held in Nagpur, it was estimated that 80 per cent of the delegates had been involved in the R.S.S. when in high school, and the R.S.S. head, M.S. Golwalkar, received a warm welcome when he attended some of the Parishad sessions. R.S.S. leaders look on the Parishad as an arm of the Hindu nationalist movement and feel that its work is valuable in making the college students aware of the nationalist movement.[32]

The Parishad has been involved in student politics to a limited extent. When the university raised its fees in 1964, the Parishad was in the forefront of an agitational effort to force the university to rescind its action. Although it was unsuccessful in this attempt, more than 10,000 signatures were collected on a petition to the Vice Chancellor. The organization was more successful at the S.N.D.T. Women's University in Bombay, where a successful agitation was staged which culminated in a strike which was 80 per cent effective.

For the past several years, the Vidyarthi Parishad has sponsored study circles which have proved fairly successful. These sessions, which have been held fortnightly on a fairly regular basis, have consisted mostly of lectures by faculty members on topics of interest to the students. Both educational and public issues have been considered by these groups.

[31] Interview with Acharya, *loc cit*.
[32] "The More Important Youth Festival in Nagpur", *Organizer*, December 7, 1964. p. 6.

The leadership of the Vidyarthi Parishad seems to be sincerely dedicated to the organization, and unlike many of the other student groups, not primarily involved in student politics for personal reasons. Moreover, the Parishad has a conscious program to train new leadership in order to provide an ongoing movement. This farsightedness has reaped benefits already, for the organization has a number of qualified younger people who have been taking an active role in the group. It is interesting, however, that the people presently in policy-making roles in the Parishad are not students but are either younger faculty members or professionals who were in the organization as students and who have stayed in active roles.

The continuing strength of the right-wing student movement is an indication of the viability of traditional ideas in India. The Vidyarthi Parishad's appeal to Hindu ideals and patriotism, the strength of rightist elements within the Congress itself, and the slow but clear growth of the R.S.S. since its debacle in 1948, are all unmistakable trends in Indian politics. It is not the specifically conservative political ideologies of these groups which attract students, but their reliance on Hindu nationalism and traditions. In a modernizing culture, there are strong elements which find it convenient to fall back on traditional values and customs rather than laboriously grapple with the new phenomena which confront society. Sections of the middle class, which has been economically pressurized from many sides in recent years, and some of the middle peasantry, who are afraid of losing their hold over the countryside in any agrarian reform program, are among these elements. Furthermore, Hindu nationalism seems to offer a way for India to get rid of the corruption and apathy which have become so widespread.

Student Agitation—1947-1965

The student movement has been relatively quiet in Bombay since 1947. Yet, a number of events of importance to the student movement and to politics in general have taken place in the period since Independence. By an examination of a few of these events, it will be possible to see how the role of the student movement changed after 1947 and how the students responded to their environment in this period.

When several of Bombay's medical colleges raised their fees by 75 per cent in 1948, there was an immediate outcry from the medical students; an *ad hoc* committee was formed to make representation to the school administrators involved and to the Health Minister. The students drew up a list of demands which included a reduction of the fee increase, more hostels for students, and better living conditions. When the demands of the students were dismissed by the authorities, the medical students' committee took the matter to the existing student organizations in Bombay at that time, the Bombay Students' Union and the Students' Congress. Student support was given to the actions of the action committee of the medical students, and conference of medical students from all over Bombay State was called. At this meeting, a long and thoughtful statement was passed, outlining some concrete proposals for the improvement of medical education in Bombay, and motions were passed demanding that the fee increase be rescinded.[33]

An agitational campaign was launched by the action committee with the support of the major student organizations in Bombay in late December, 1948. Students picketed the college principal's office and the accountant's office. Students in Bombay and Poona went on a hunger strike. When the condition of the hunger strikers became serious after six days without food, the Bombay Students' Union and the Students' Congress called a strike of all students in Bombay, and on January 6, 1949, 10,000 students left their classes to support the medical students.[34]

The protest against the medical fee increase was successfully organized by student political groups yet, it was never transformed from a legitimate campus issue into a political question, and although the action taken by the students reached dramatic proportions, the only aim was a reduction in medical school fees. This limitation of the issue was possible to a great extent because outside political forces remained aloof from the conflict. The strike which took place at the Victoria Jubilee Technical Institute (V.J.T.I.) in 1949 is an example of a pro-

[33] *Bombay Chronicle*, December 7, 1948, p. 7.
[34] *Bombay Chronicle*, January 1, 1949, p.. 3.

test which started as a campus issue and was transformed, in this case by the Communist Bombay Students' Union into a political campaign against the Congress movement. The V.J.T.I. agitation was ultimately unsuccessful.

The V.J.T.I. crisis came at the height of the "adventurist" period of Indian Communism; at that time, the B.S.U. was interested in creating as many embarrassing issues for the government as possible, in order to prove its essentially "reactionary" nature.

Discontent at V.J.T.I., which stemmed from the admittedly poor living conditions to which the students at the Institute were subjected, was first crystallized and organized when students living in the Institute's hostel formed an action committee to present their grievances to the principal. At an open meeting at which many of the V.J.T.I. students were present, a number of criticisms of the administration were made and a set of demands were drawn up to be presented to the principal. From the beginning the several Bombay Students' Union members in key positions among the student body worked hard to make the student demands as radical as possible so as to cause the maximum amount of disruption.

Much to everyone's surprise, the principal responded to the students' demands by ordering them to stop their demonstrations and strikes or face severe consequences. Angered by this response, the students increased their struggle. During the V.J.T.I. agitation, the action committee approached the various student organizations in Bombay for help. The Communist Bombay Students' Union took up the cause immediately and turned it into a mass campaign. On two occasions, the entire student community in Bombay struck for one day in support of the V.J.T.I. students, and student mobs attacked V.J.T.I. property.[35] The B.S.U. leadership, after it had succeeded in launching a mass agitation, was not interested in a compromise but wanted to keep the struggle at a high pitch.

The agitational campaigns which took place between 1947 and 1965 concerning fee increases and examinations have both political and educational overtones. These agitations, which were occasionally, although not usually, successful, involved

[35] *Bombay Chronicle*, October 1, 1949, p. 11.

students from various different student organizations at various times and in differing kinds of activity. When the university raised examination fees in 1947, the Students' Congress issued a number of statements in opposition to this action, and threatened to strike in order to support its demands. The educational authorities stood firm, however, and the students went on strike. More than 50,000 stayed out of classes for one day as a protest. They also collected funds to help poor students and tried to start a textbook library. Although a good deal of discontent was shown by the students, there was no violence.

When college and school fees were raised again in 1948, the Bombay Students' Union took up the issue and called a one day strike against the university's decision.[36] The B.S.U. called on the university to immediately reverse their decision, but it also asked the government to provide more support for higher education and to give special grants to night school students. When students invaded the university senate, four were arrested, although the university again stood firm in its position and fees continued at the level set by the administration. Other fee increase agitations took place in 1950 and intermittantly during the following period.

Other demonstrations also took place during this period. When a popular secondary school teacher was fired, high school students went on a strike which affected twenty-five schools in Bombay, demanding that the teacher be reinstated. Later, the teachers' union also sponsored a demonstration, and the teacher was re-admitted after some discussion.[37] Sindhi students at one of Bombay's colleges struck when the Sindhi language was removed from curriculum, and secondary and college students struck several times over issues of the Secondary School Certificate Examination, which was always a point of controversy between the university (which administered the tests) and the student community.

Despite these demonstrations, which were usually peaceful in nature and seldom successful, the period under consideration was relatively quiet. Certainly, the agitations of this

[36] *Bombay Chronicle*, July 24, 1948, p. 12.
[37] *Bombay Chronicle*, August 23, 1951, p. 8.

period did not get the broad student support of the pre-Independence period.[38]

In one agitation, which lasted only a few hours, the students residing in one of the college dormitories in Bombay protested the imposition of what were considered unfair hours by spontaneously walking out of their hostel and marching to the house of the principal and demanding that he explain his action. When the principal refused to meet with a student delegation, frustration increased. Finally, after standing quietly in a street for several hours, several hundred students returned to their hostel when the principal relented and agreed to reconsider the issue. The agitation proved successful when the hour restriction was lifted a few days later. These unimportant incidents are indicative of the present trend in student activity in Bombay. It has been said that there is a good deal of frustration among the students, but this frustration is seldom translated into any kind of action, either constructive or destructive.

The Morning College Question—Education and Politics in the 1960s

One of the few issues which raised controversy among both educators and politicians was the question about the "morning colleges". This issue, which was raised by the student organizations and in which students have taken an active interest, has not yet been completely resolved.

The roots of the morning college agitation go back to the late 1930s, when increasing demands on the colleges and classrooms necessitated that facilities be expanded to meet these challanges. At that time, Bombay University permitted Khalsa College to schedule classes in the morning as well as in the afternoon, thus creating a "morning college". This arrangement also permitted students to hold full-time jobs as well as attend college. This gave rise to the "earner-learner", who has become an established part of Bombay's system of higher education. In addition to allowing the colleges to almost double their enrollments, the university made college education possible for large numbers of lower middle class or working class

---
[38] Interview with Bhansali, *loc. cit.*

students. The morning colleges, which were started as a temporary arrangement, have functioned since the late 1930s almost continuously because the educational system has never been relieved of the pressure of expanding numbers.

The arguments concerning the morning college have centered around several critical issues. The formation of the colleges was considered an expedient measure by the university administration, which noted the academic drawbacks of the system. The senate was also reluctant to undertake any measure which would diminish the already limited corporate life of the colleges. The university authorities noted that the students attending the morning classes would spend less time on the college premises, and would have less time to study since many held outside jobs. There were, however, many spokesmen for the morning colleges, including most of the student organizations and many independent intellectuals in Bombay. It was claimed by this group that the morning colleges would allow poorer students the opportunity to obtain a college education, a hitherto undreamt of achievement.

The institution of morning classes in the downtown colleges was an extremely important innovation, since it allowed many young people who held jobs in the business area to attend morning classes and still arrive at their jobs at the proper time. Thus, there was a rapid increase in the morning college enrolment. This influx also proved a financial boon for the colleges involved.

In later years, when the morning colleges were under attack, it was charged that these colleges made a substantial profit from the morning classes. Science degrees were not given on the basis of morning college attendance, so the arts classes were heavily involved in this arrangement.

With a rapid expansion of Bombay's institutions of higher education during the 1950s and 1960s, the university administration, and particularly the rector, G. D. Parikh, felt that the time had come to close the morning colleges. The rector produced a memorandum entitled *Reorganization of Undergraduate Teaching in Arts* in 1961, and the morning college issue was discussed in the university senate.[39] Parikh's argu-

[39] G. D. Parikh, *Reorganization of Undergraduate Teaching in Arts* (Bombay: Bombay University Press, 1961).

ments centered mainly around the academic failings of the morning colleges and claimed that the students attending these classes received an inferior education and that many non-working students were taking advantage of the situation. Parikh went on to state that since the colleges affiliated to Bombay University had facilities for all students, the morning colleges, which had been set up as a temporary measure, should be abolished. He proposed that working students should have an option to attend classes in the evening, but that their course of study should be six years instead of the usual four.

These proposals received immediate attention from the educational community as well as from the public. The students, while generally in favour of retaining the morning classes, did not speak out vehemently on the subject at this time. Many educators agreed with the rector, as did much of the press. There were, however, a good many critics who strongly favored the morning classes. The Bombay Students' Union issued a memorandum which stated that the examination results showed that morning college students did as well as their day school colleagues and that there was less indiscipline among them. It claimed that the sinking standards of higher education in Bombay were not due to the morning colleges, but to other, more general conditions within the society and the educational system. Much of the dissention was caused by the fact that the rector was involved in a feud with some members of the university senate, and used the morning college issue to obtain support for his own views.[40]

When the senate voted in 1961 to abolish the morning colleges, the students called a march on the Legislative Assembly to demand government support for the morning colleges. While the demonstration was not an overwhelming success, a letter was delivered to the Minister of Education which set forth the arguments for the morning colleges, and leading politicians were made aware of the issue. The students claimed that a six-year course was an unfair handicap for the poorer students, and that standards at the morning colleges did in fact remain at reasonably high levels. A City Students' Action Committee was set up in September of 1961 to deal with the

[40] Interview with Namjoshi, *loc. cit.*

problems and several public meetings were held to bring attention to the issue.⁴¹ In the meantime, the university authorities went ahead with plans to abolish the morning classes.

The National Union of Students in Bombay

One of the major post-Independence efforts to create a nonpartizan student movement in India was the National Union of Students. Founded in 1950 by a combination of Congress and Socialist student groups, the N.U.S. had the blessings of such figures as Nehru and Jayaprakash Narayan. The hopes of many students were pinned on the success of the N.U.S., which many saw as the logical extension of the student movement of the Independence struggle. The inaugural session of the National Union of Students was held in Bombay, and was indicative of the organization's future. The enthusiasm of many of the student delegates, who came from all parts of India, was dampened by poor planning and by political factionalism. Interference from Communist students, and internal disputes between supporters of the Congress and the Socialists marred the proceedings.

The National Union of Students proved a disappointment in almost every respect. It was unable to build up a mass following, and in most areas students were not actively involved in the organization. Opposition from university administrators, and meddling from politicians marked the organization's progress. While the N.U.S. continued to function in many areas for a few years, it never became a truly national movement, and it gradually lost the support which it had originally claimed. The organization died a natural death in the late 1950s, and not since the Independence struggle has a national student organization been able to function in India.

Bombay was a key testing ground for the National Union of Students. Its national office was located in Bombay, and its president was also from that city.

The problems which faced the N.U.S. in Bombay were of an all-India nature. Bombay's colleges were widely scattered, making communication and coordination difficult and ineffici-

⁴¹ Interview with Arvind Phansekar, Secretary, Vidyarthi Mandal (Worli), January 17, 1965.

ent. There was no university student union to act as a coordinating body for the local college unions, for the administration of the university was hostile to any notions of increased student self-government or integration. Furthermore, many of the local college unions were not democratically elected, while others were subjected to much administrative interference.

Much of the energy of the N.U.S. in Bombay was expended in trying to bridge the communications gap between the students in the colleges. Debates, lectures, and cultural events were organized on an all-Bombay basis. These events were by and large well attended. Debates were held on many topics, such as "should students participate in politics", "India's food problem cannot be solved without family planning", and others. Occasionally, professors debated with groups of students, thereby bringing these two rather distant groups into closer contact. Symposia on university reforms and the examination system gave students a chance to air their views on those topics. A number of lectures were sponsored by the N.U.S. on a variety of topics.

One of the most interesting ideas promoted by the N.U.S. was the Bombay Students' Medical Scheme. This project, originated by the N.U.S. President, Dr. Shallat, proposed to set up clinics where students could receive inexpensive medical treatment and drugs at a discount. The need for such a program was evident, since many students went without adequate food and medical attention. The scheme received the support of a number of hospitals and government health authorities. Although plans were made and the scheme inaugurated in a ceremony which featured the Health Minister, it was doomed to failure for lack of efficient management and sustained interest from both the hospitals and the N.U.S. administraters. The Medical Scheme, like so many of the N.U.S.'s activities,— cooperative book stores for students and libraries—proved abortive.

One of the most useful aspects of N.U.S. work in Bombay was the sponsorship of inexpensive educational and sightseeing tours. In 1952, sixty-five Bombay college students visited Kashmir and northern India. During this visit they had the opportunity to meet the President of India and to visit students from other universities in India. However, this tour was badly organized and engendered a good deal of negative comment from the participants, who accused the N.U.S. officers of misappropriating their money and of general inefficiency. The Bombay N.U.S. sponsored other, less ambitious and more successful, educational tours, some of which brought students from other cities to visit Bomaby.

One of the original emphases of the N.U.S. was on social service and nation-building. The N.U.S. in Bombay sponsored a number of social service projects during its first few years of existence. In 1951, the N.U.S. sponsored a six-week social service program, half of which was devoted to a series of lectures and classes, and the other half to village work applying these academic insights. In 1952, thirty-five students participated in a two-week project near Poona, and built three miles of road. Other projects involved several hundred students per year in village-based social service projects. These projects proved popular, for students were willing to donate time and energy.

In Bombay, the N.U.S. interest in politics was restricted to student-oriented issues. When the Government of Bombay raised college fees, the N.U.S. adamantly opposed this, and sent deputations to government officials, threatening agitation on the subject. In the end, the government was persuaded to rescind its order, eliminating the need for direct action from the students.

The National Union of Students in Bombay never was able to become a mass-based student movement as its organizers had planned. It gathered representatives from twenty-six of Bombay's colleges to sit on its council, but there was a good deal of fluctuation of membership, and many of the colleges showed scant interest in the functioning of the council. Moreover, the college representatives often did not even report on N.U.S. activities to their local constituencies, thereby effectively shutting off communications. The N.U.S. secretariat claimed that 10,000 of Bombay's 45,000 students were members of the N.U.S. in 1952, though this figure seems overly optimistic.[42]

By 1955, it became clear that the N.U.S. was not, in fact,

---

[42] National Union of Students, "Letter to the *Free Press Journal*" (Mimeographed, in the files of the National Union of Students).

a representative student organization in Bombay but merely one of many student groups then struggling on the verge of collapse. After 1955, the N.U.S. program in Bombay was practically non-existent. Even its national office, which continued to operate out of St. Xavier's College, was moribund. Funds were short, and the Bombay secretary reported that recruiting members and collecting dues, a very nominal one rupee twenty cents) per year, was quite difficult. Originally, it was hoped that students would automatically join the N.U.S. upon registration at their colleges, but the college authorities did not agree to this procedure, and the N.U.S. was forced to engage in usually unsuccessful membership drives.

A report of the Executive Committee of the Bombay branch of the N.U.S., issued in 1951, gives some valuable insights into the problems of the organization. The report stated that the political differences among the students were a great hinderance to the organization's functioning, causing disrupted meetings and a lack of agreement on basic policy issues. The hostility of the college principals and of the Education Department of Bombay state toward the N.U.S., greatly hindered the work of the organization. The committee concluded that the N.U.S. had great potential, but that, even in 1951, it was faced with substantial problems which only hard work and initiative would overcome.[43]

As it became clear that the N.U.S. was having serious problems, and as the organization itself made serious blunders, criticism grew among educators and the public. An editorial in the *Free Press Journal* attacked the N.U.S. for mishandling several activities and for misrepresenting its size and influence. The editorial also said that the N.U.S. was misappropriating funds and was not a legitimate student organization. The secretary of the organization wrote an irate letter to the paper, but did not refute the charges very effectively.[44]

Many of the reasons for the failure of the National Union of Students in Bombay have been alluded to in the foregoing discussion. Sporadic political interference combined with the

[43] National Union of Students, *Report on the State of the N.U.S. in Bombay* (Bombay: National Union of Students, 1951), p. 4.
[44] National Union of Students, "Letter" to the *Free Press Journal, op. cit.*

steady indifference of political leaders, hostility from educators and college principals, and a student body more interested in its own problems and careers than in building a movement combined to defeat the efforts to create a student movement in post-Independence Bombay. A lack of leadership plagued the organization throughout its existence, and no real attempts were made by the founding officers of the N.U.S. to provide for ongoing leadership. Officers were intent on keeping their own positions as long as possible, to obtain overseas trips and other benefits. Several N.U.S. officers continued to hold office long after they had ceased to be students.

Non-Political Student Activity since 1947

Agitational issues have failed to arouse the student support that they did prior to 1947, and the student community has been characterized by quietism, if not apathy. Because of this undeniable change in the student movement, student cultural and social activities have taken on more importance for the student community.

Among the most active groups on any college campus are the various linguistic societies formed by the college. Groups like the Marathi Literary Society, the Gujarati Circle, the Sindhi Circle, and similar organizations are quite popular among the students and have well established traditions dating back several decades. These groups are among the few socially acceptable ways of meeting students of the opposite sex, and give the students a chance to relax in familiar surroundings.

These groups have official sponsorship and often receive small grants of money from the college for their activities. Their programs usually include dramatic productions in the language of the group, an annual picnic at some park, several lectures on community or language problems or issues by a prominent local leader from the community in question. There is often a high prestige attached to heading these groups, and they do provide the valuable service of giving the students who are not particularly fluent in English (and their numbers are growing), a place to feel secure and to express themselves with their fellow students. They occasionally publish small journals which feature original writing by the students in their mother tongue.

The fact that Bombay is a cosmopolitan center and that it contains many minority groups makes these groups even more important, for they provide a center of identity for a large number of students who would otherwise be lost in unfamiliar surroundings. Organizations for students from Kerala, Bengal, Madras, as well as large Marathi and Gujarati groups exist at most of the colleges. These linguistic groups, although mutually exclusive, do not seem to have divided the student community in any way. The linguistic groups have, however, tended to cut down the never substantial amount of social contact between students of differing linguistic and ethnic backgrounds.

Stemming from the British emphasis on debating, the Indian student community has always followed debating competitions avidly, and good debators have always been held in high esteem by their peers. Bombay has a long tradition of debating competitions, dating from the early part of the present century. The missionary colleges used to encourage the students to become proficient in debating in the English language, and St. Xavier's College established a well known debating trophy early in the century over which the various colleges held an annual competition.

Theater involves a small but active group of students in Bombay. There are various outlets for the theatrically inclined students in Bombay. The Indian National Theater was started by students, as was People's Theater movement in the 1940s. In addition, drama groups exist at many of the colleges. Occasionally the dramatic efforts are produced in English, but more often in one of the Indian languages. Both modern and traditional drama is produced, and some of it reaches a fairly high level. Drama is one of the few activities in which boys and girls can participate together without too much embarrassment.

Related to both the theater programs and to debating, in a sense, have been the mock parliaments which many of the colleges have sponsored since Independence. These activities, which are often quite elaborate and well organized, involve students who are interested in politics in a series of debates and discussions on national issues in a setting as much like the Indian parliament as is possible. As some of Bombay's colleges, such as Siddharth College, mock parliaments have a long tradition, and are quite elaborately prepared and executed. At Siddharth, there are a number of political parties which closely resemble the parties in national Indian politics. These parties hold an election campaign, complete with speeches, posters, and leaflets, and on the basis of this election, in which all of the students in the college are eligible to participate, the number of seats in the parliament are distributed.[45] The Siddharth College parliament has proved quite successful over the years and has provided many students with valuable training and has raised the level of political interest among the students without creating any "indiscipline" or other adverse effects.

St. Xavier's College instituted an interesting experiment in student participation in college affairs during the mid-1950s. The experiment, called "Xavierland," was an attempt to let the students, through elected representatives, debate issues concerning the college administration and their own education as well as national issues. One of the main obstacles to these mock parliaments have been the attitude of many college principals, who are afraid to allow the students a place to air their views. Although where the parliament programs have been instituted, there have been no problems, many administrators are not willing to experiment.

Athletic programs have existed in Bombay colleges for many years, although there has never been a strong tradition of intercollegiate competition. However, various colleges do compete in some forms of athletics. Most colleges do not require athletic training for the students, and the facilities which most possess are inadequate. Many of the colleges in Bombay have no facilities for athletic activity. Bombay University's own facilities are inadequate for all of the colleges. In recent years, male students have been required to undergo several years of military training as a part of their education. This training, however, has not proved particularly popular, nor has it been very successful, mainly because of the poor quality of instruction. In any case, this occasional military training does not provide much physical exercise.

[45] Interview with Dandavate, *loc. cit.*

Students in Bombay have also occasionally participated in social service work in addition to their studies in the colleges. Only a small minority of the student community participates in any kind of social service work. There is a good deal of cynicism, much of it justified, about the constructive value of such work, and many of the social service projects in the past have been administered very badly.

Many of the groups engaged in social service work have been directly connected with one or another political party, thereby limiting their attraction to many students and making cooperation with the local college authorities difficult. The Congress sponsored group, the Congress Seva Dal (Congress Service Organization), has been almost totally ineffective. The Rashtra Seva Dal, which has been mentioned earlier, is one of the few groups which has been moderately successful in arousing student support, although it has loose socialist affiliations. One group which has successfully planned and executed social service projects in recent years, the Bharat Sevak Samaj (Indian Service Society), has only involved several hundred students per year in its activities, although its organizers have stated that many more students would be willing to participate if there were adequate programs.[46] This group, which is a private voluntary association, has projects in villages and rural areas as well as in the slums of Bombay, and provides trained social workers to supervise the students.

The decline of interest in social service activity among the students has many causes. The fact that many students are from lower middle and working class backgrounds means that they simply do not have the time to participate in such activities. Moreover, the social service organizations themselves have been involved in political disputes, and have lost much of their support in recent years. In addition, the whole ethos of the student community seems to have changed. While the influence of Gandhian concepts of service motivated students in the 1940s and many others were interested in propagating political ideas among villagers, both of these motivations are lacking at the present time. It is true, however, that well orga-

[46] Interview with N. B. Chaudhary, Zonal Organizer, Bharat Sevak Samaj, October 28, 1964.

nized and publicized social service projects have received relatively enthusiastic support from the students, indicating that there is a basis of idealism, since these camps characteristically offer few chances for publicity or personal advancement.

Conclusions

There are several generalizations that can be drawn from the foregoing discussion. The causes of the new trends in student activity are both intricate and complex; yet, these trends must be thoroughly analyzed and understood before India can begin to solve the pressing problems facing higher education in Bombay and other cities.

The almost complete collapse of the student movement as it was known prior to Independence was the most dramatic fact of the present period. The transformation of the nationalist movement into a political machine, and the withdrawal of support from the student movement by this machine not only demoralized the students, but took away one of the main legitimizing factors behind the movement. The end of the Independence struggle brought an end to the spirit of sacrifice and ideological warfare which had accompanied it. In short, the student political movement lost its political *raison d'etre*, and the powers in society did everything possible to discourage the continued existence of a militant and ideologically aware student community. It is also true that the ethos of personal gain and concern for the individual rather than the society pervaded the student community after 1947, just as it did the rest of Indian society.

The educational system was also in a period of transition, and the changes which were taking place did not present favorable conditions for the flourishing of active student movements. The increasing diffusion of college education to various social classes and the more geographical spread of the colleges made effective organizational work more difficult. Many students who attended the morning colleges simply had no time to participate in the student movement. Others, coming from the less secure lower middle classes, were unwilling to risk a future job by participating in politics. Teachers, also ceased to support the movement.

Non-political aspects of the student movement also lost some of their vitality during this period. As students became disillusioned with the movement, they often did not differentiate between the groups involved, and abstained from all student activity, and not just from the political groups. In addition, the college and university administrators did not usually differentiate between political and cultural groups, and most student organizations were frowned upon unless they were under the direct control of the principal. Students, also, could generally spare less time from their jobs or personal affairs.

Student agitational activity during this period swung from its emphasis on political affairs and the broader issues of society to almost a total emphasis on educational issues, often of a rather unimportant nature. "Student indiscipline" has been a relatively rare phenomenon in Bombay, when compared with such cities as Calcutta, Delhi, and Banares. Although the nature of some of the agitational activity in Bombay since 1947 indicates that many students are alienated from the educational system and from their teachers, there has been no continuing movement.

One of the most acute problems for student activity in Bombay has been leadership. The prestige which once went with student leadership, particularly in the political area, has disappeared, and while student leaders used to come from the highest academic levels, they now show little academic distinction. The lack of leadership, caused by a general dearth of student political activity, decreasing prestige, the tendency for the most intelligent students to choose the exacting fields of science and the professions, and other factors, has helped to destroy the student movement. As a result, student "indiscipline" in the 1960's tends to be sporadic and leaderless.

In a real sense, there is no student movement in Bombay in the mid-1960s, if by student movement one means a definable set of independent student organizations devoted to any social goal. The student movement has been destroyed by the trend of political life in India, and by the attitude of both educators and government officials, who have attempted to stifle the organization of independent student associations. Because these independent student organizations have not been replaced by other forms of student activity, there now exists same thing of a vacuum on the campus. The rather sporadic incidents of student "indiscipline" are a function of this lack of direction and the organizational vacuum among students in Bombay.

PART III
ASPECTS OF STUDENTS AND POLITICS
SOME CASE STUDIES

CHAPTER VIII

COMMUNAL STUDENT ORGANIZATIONS
THE MUSLIMS AS A CASE STUDY

It is clear that the deep linguistic, religious, and caste divisions which exist in Indian society have played an important role in shaping the student movement. Bombay is a particularly good place to study these various communities, for the city contains many diverse groups. Because of its prominence as an industrial and financial center, Bombay has attracted people from all over the subcontinent; subsequently, over the years, substantial communities of Bengalis, Tamlians, Sikhs, and many other groups have settled in the city. A number of Bombay's colleges have been endowed by these groups.

The student community has also been affected by these groups. Students are naturally aware of their linguistic and religious communities, and there are often strong social pressures to identify closely with them, often to the exclusion of other contacts. Marriage is almost universally expected to take place within the community. The nationalist student movement, although professing non-communal ideologies and often making efforts to break down linguistic and religious antagonism, was also affected by these important communal differences.

The Muslim community in Bombay is both large and influential. Muslims constitute about 15 per cent of Bombay's population. While most Muslims are both poor and uneducated, some have enjoyed higher education, and there is a sizable Muslim elite in the city which has made important contributions to Muslims life in India. The Muslims in India have been a key minority group. Though internally divided along community lines, the Muslims dominated the political and cultural life of the subcontinent under the Moguls, and left their mark on India's cultural heritage.

Muslim student groups have existed in Bombay since the beginning of the twentieth century. Since the Muslim community was comparatively backward, the student groups played a particularly important role in helping to provide socialization to Western and modern Indian values. These associations were able to take an active part in the politics of the Muslim community and to provide leadership. The most important Muslim leader in twentieth century India, Mohammad Ali Jinnah, was a product of the Muslim Students' union in Bombay. Other Muslim leaders now prominent in both India and Pakistan also come from the Muslim student groups of the 1920's and 1930's. These groups gave students uninitiated in Western ideas a chance to discuss mutual problems in small groups. Although it is true that most of the communal student organizations, Muslim and others, did not take part in ideological politics as the Congress and the Communists did, they sometimes participated in the political life of the nation, providing their members with a political orientation, if not a specific ideology.

The Muslim Students' Union

The oldest and most important of the Muslim student groups is the Muslim Students' Union, which has existed for more than half a century. With the exception of a short period in the early 1940's, when the organization activity joined with the Muslim League in its attempts to apply pressure for the creation of Pakistan, the Muslim Students' Union served an essentially non-political function. It existed as a focus for the activities of the Muslim student community. It also provided financial support for needy Muslim students, and still provides free books for some poor students. The fact that it has survived so long is impressive.

According to its Annual Report of 1920, the aims and objects of the Muslim Students' Union were :

1. To provide facilities for social intercourse between students of various colleges and schools and also to offer them opportunities for coming in touch with leading men of the older generation.
2. To establish and maintain a spirit of cooperation and brotherhood among the different sections of the Muslim community.

3. To foster and strengthen the cause of the unity between Muslim students and those of other communities.
4. To promote and encourage literary pursuits and to develop elocutionary power of the student members.
5. To otherwise provide for the mental, moral and material welfare of Muslim students in general.[1]

The organization's rules went on to state that the Muslim Students' Union would always keep out of "actual and administrative politics." The M.S.U. was one of the few student organizations in Bombay which was able to afford its own premises, and was even able to provide a tennis court for the use of the students. The offices of the Union were located in a non-Muslim middle class area of Bombay, thereby affording increased contact with the outside world. Students not connected with the Union, even non-Muslim students, took advantage of these offices, and were almost always welcomed by the M.S.U. members.

During the period prior to 1930, a large proportion of the Union's activities were social or cultural. During the 1921-22 school year, for instance, seven lectures were arranged, which were attended mainly by outsiders. Elocution competitions were quite successful, and various "conversational meetings", informal discussions, were held during the year. Debates also played a role in the programming of the Union and occasionally attracted large crowds. The level of activity of the Union, as well as its membership, varied from year to year, depending on the specific composition of the managing committee and the enthusiasm of the membership.

During the 1920s and early 1930s the leadership of the Union helped to extend education to the Muslim population, which was seen to be backward and in need of special help. Efforts were made to interest young people in education, and some scholarship aid was given to needy students.

Another contribution of the Union was its advocacy of the abolition of purdah, and its encouragement of women's rights. Muslim college girls, who were in a small minority, were en-

[1] Muslim Students' Union, *Rules and Regulations* (Bombay: Muslim Students' Union, 1920), p. 1.

couraged to come to M.S.U. meetings, and because the headquarters were in a non-Muslim area, it was possible for girls to shed their veils, a radical action at that time. Participation in Union activities gave college girls self-confidence. The backwardness of Muslim women in Bombay is indicated by the fact that the first female graduate of the Bohra Muslim community finished her college education in 1941. Since then, partly due to the efforts of the Union, the number of Muslim girls in Bombay colleges has increased greatly.

The Muslim Students' Union attracted the best of the Muslim students in Bombay, and helped to train some of the leading figures in Muslim life in the city. In addition to Jinnah, the former Minister of Education of India, M. C. Chagla, served as president of the Union for a number of years. Yusuf Meherally was also active in the organization during its early period.

The Union also provided a valuable forum for ambitious young Muslims to obtain leadership training and to attract the attention of influential members of the Muslim and broader communities in Bombay. The various competitions and debates brought able students to the lime-light, and gave them needed publicity. One of the purposes of the organization was to develop leadership in the Muslim community, and to provide direction for its young people.[2a]

Muslim Communalism vs. Indian Nationalism: the Student Response

As the nationalist movement grew in strength and the political situation in India changed radically, the Muslim community and the student movement also underwent changes. The "honeymoon" of Hindu-Muslim cooperation which had existed during the early history of the Congress ended when Jinnah and his followers gradually articulated the idea of a separate political identity for the Indian Muslims. As Independence neared, the call of the Muslim League, which had the support of a majority of Indian Muslims, was for an independent Pakistan. These extremely important political currents and

[2a] Interview with Salim Merchant, former Secretary, Muslim Students' Union, March 22, 1965.

events could not but have a profound impact on the Muslim students of India.

During the 1930's both nationalists and communalists courted the Muslim Students' Union actively, since the League and the Congress saw the Union as an important segment of the Muslim community. Both Jinnah and Nehru spoke to the Union on several occasions and asked for the loyalty of the Muslim students. The Union allowed speakers from the opposing groups to speak freely. In addition to these politically oriented activities, the Union collected funds for earthquake victims in 1934 and engaged in other social service projects during this period. Social and cultural programs were also continued actively, and the M.S.U. constituted one of the few cases of non-political activity in an increasingly militant student community. The occasion of the Silver Jubilee of the M.S.U. in 1941 aroused a good deal of interest from the citizens of Bombay, and from a number of leading political figures. Gandhi, who had spoken under the auspices of the Union in the past, sent a message saying, "I do hope that your celebrations will succeed and that your effort will bring about communal harmony."[2b] Other nationalist leaders also took the opportunity to plead for communal unity. M.S.U. leaders emphasized that students should not take part in "controversial politics", although a generally nationalist approach was taken at the anniversary celebrations.[3]

In the struggle for control of the Muslim Students' Union, the nationalist forces put up a stiff fight, even though it was fairly obvious, by the late 1930s, that they were a distinct minority among Muslims in Bombay. The nationalist Muslims felt that the best that they could accomplish in the student movement was to keep the Muslim groups neutral and effectively out of the political struggle. They, therefore, worked hard to keep the M.S.U. non-political and were successful in this attempt until 1943. Thus, even the non-political nature of the Union was at least partially a function of the political struggle at the time.[4]

[2b] *Free Press Journal*, January 28, 1941, p. 4.
[3] *Evening News*, January 27, 1941, p. 8.
[4] Interview with Merchant, *loc. cit.*

Pro-League students, frustrated in their attempts to control the Muslim Students' Union (which would have been a prize because of its financial stability and long traditions), proceeded to form their own organization, the Bombay Presidency Muslim Students' Federation. This organization served virtually the same function that the nationalist and Communist student organizations did, though for different purposes. The Fedration was started by the Muslim League in 1937 in order to provide a student front for the Muslim cause. At its founding conference in 1937, M. A. Jinnah spoke of the need for a seperate anti-Congress Muslim student movement, and won the support of a majority of the delegates.[5] Somewhat later, a pro-nationalist All-India Nationalist Muslim Students' Federation was formed, but this group did not have much support among Muslim students. The *Bombay Chronicle* started :

> That the Bombay Muslim Students' Federation has been established unanimously last Sunday is a fact which its few detractors conveniently overlook. The sincerity and ability of those who supported the move will be justified by the success which the Federation is bound to achieve. The popularity and support vouchsafed to it in various districts is its sufficient justification and *raison d'etre*. That there must be for social, cultural and academic purposes a common bond of union between the Muslim students of various districts cannot be challenged.[6]

The article went on to attack the nationalist Muslims for deserting their community and raising a false bogey of communalism. It was clear that the split in the Muslim ranks caused a good deal of bitterness and hostility between the two groups. The Federation acted as an arm of the Muslim League, and helped with League propaganda work in the Muslim areas of Bombay. When the British permitted elections, Muslim student members of the Federation were key campaign workers for the Muslim League. Among the students, the Federation tried to counteract the influence of the nationalist movement in general and the nationalist Muslims in particular. The Federation had the

---
[5] Reddy, *op. cit.*, p. 72.
[6] *Bombay Chronicle*, May 8, 1945, p. 6.

support of a majority of the Muslim college students in Bombay, and was able to continue functioning even when the nationalist student organizations in Bombay were banned by the British authorities in 1942.[7] Unlike the Union, which had a small but active membership drawn from the elite of the Muslim student community, the Federation had a mass membership but little commitment from individual members. Several of the leaders of the Federation, however, later became leaders in Pakistan after leaving Bombay in 1948.[8]

The Bombay Muslim Students' Federation reached the height of its influence in 1942-43, when it took over the Muslim Students' Union. At this time, which coincided with the heat of the nationalist struggle, the Federation conducted an active propaganda campaign with the support of a majority of the Muslim student population. The nationalists were forced out of the Muslim Students' Union, and constitutional changes were adopted which gave the organization a specifically political tone. Among the objectives of the organization were:

1. To arouse the political consciousness amongst the Muslim students and to prepare them to take their proper share in the struggle for the attainment of Pakistan.
2. To organize the Muslim students of Bombay city and suburbs into a corporate body and to safeguard the interests of the Muslim student community....
3. To popularize the study of Islamic culture and to combat the propaganda against the faith carried on by anti-Islamic forces.[9]

The nationalist Muslims, though a minority, did not passively accept defeat in the Muslim Students' Union. Instead, they started their own organization, the Bombay Provincial Muslim Youth Federation, as a counter-weight to the League's organizational efforts. This group had little following and was not very active, although it did keep up the pretense that the

[7] Interview with Ashrafali Q. Jairazbhoy, former president of the Muslim Students' Union, February 1, 1966.
[8] *Ibid.*
[9] Muslim Students' Union, *Thirty-First Annual Report* (Bombay: Muslim Students' Union, 1947), p. 2.

Congress had wide support from all communities. The nationalists did their best to stem the League tide, but were, in the last analysis, unsuccessful.

The Muslim student organizations tried to keep up a program of social service work during this period, even though the atmosphere was highly political. The literacy work began by the Muslim Students' Union was continued by the Federation, as was counselling for prospective students, visits to slum areas, and village social work.[10] Muslim students collected funds for victims of communal rioting in Bihar in 1946, and additional funds were sent to Muslim victims of riots in a district of Bombay state.

When partition took place in 1947, many of the ardently pro-Pakistan student leaders left Bombay and settled in Pakistan. The Muslim Students' Federation went out of existence, as its *raison d'etre* was fulfilled, and many of its leaders had left India. The Muslim Students' Union, however, was not left in a strong position. The pro-League elements left a shell of an organization when they withdrew. They did, however, leave behind the office premises and the trust fund, making it possible for the Union to revive itself. Some of the adult Muslim leaders who had chosen to remain in India worked to restore the Union and were able to re-establish the Union.

Muslim Students since Independence

The Muslim Students' Union never really revived after 1947. Its organizational structure continues to exist, mainly owing to the trust fund which continues to supply a small yearly income to the organization, but its roots seem to be dead. Since Independence, the Union has engaged in practically no public activities. The lecture programs of former days are gone, as are the discussion meetings. The constitution of the organization was restored to its old, non-political form, and the Union has kept scrupulously away from politics in recent years.

The Union continues to maintain its headquarters in a Muslim area of Bombay, and serves the community by providing room

---

[10] *Bombay Chronicle*, May 8, 1945, p. 6.

for indoor games, magazines for reading, and books for poor students. The approximately 100 students who maintain membership in the organization do so primarily to take advantage of the indoor game facilities. Even the annual meeting of the Union is little more than a perfunctory election of officers. Little interest has been shown in the organization by the adult Muslim community, and prominent Muslims still living in Bombay who are alumni of the organization take almost no interest in its work.

With college education accepted as a common place for a large number of urban Indian young people, the Union's old function of "selling" higher education to Muslim boys is no longer necessary. One of the few alumni of the Union who still takes an interest in the organization and who handles its trust fund, feels that the Muslim Students' Union should go out of existence and give the remaining funds to charity.[11]

Conclusion

The general collapse of the Muslim student movement which has been seen in Bombay has been repeated all over India. Only at strongly Muslim colleges such as Aligarh Muslim University in northern India (which has seen a good deal of student unrest since 1947), have Muslim groups been able to maintain themselves. Many of the militant Muslim student leaders are no longer in India. Those Muslims who remained see no future for themselves in politics. Other Muslims are apprehensive about their future in an essentially Hindu nation and are therefore unwilling to join groups which could be considered communal by the Hindu majority. In the Indian Muslim community, there is a good deal of uncertainty about the future.

There is no doubt that developments in the broader Muslim community played an important role in the development of the Muslim student movement. The political crisis of the 1930s transformed the student organizations and gave them an entirely new direction. In the 1920s, the needs of an underdeveloped Muslim community and a real sense of responsibility by

---

[11] Interview with Jairazbhoy, *loc. cit.*

the upper class elements made the Union a primary agency for the "socialization" of Muslim young people in modern ideas. Thus, the Union became one of the primary agencies of change and modernization within the Muslim community. After Independence, the Muslim student organizations were unable to re-establish themselves owing to many factors. The general lack of direction in the Muslim community in India was partly responsible for this. The total problem of the Indian student movement also accounts for some of the difficulties encountered by the Muslims. A change in the nature of higher education in India has also been a contributing factor to the demise of the Muslim organizations. Many of the cultural functions formerly performed by the M.S.U. have been taken over by the various colleges themselves, making an outside agency unnecessary. Students are no longer as diffident about making social contacts, nor is the urban Muslim community as backward as it was.

All this is not to say that the Muslim Students' Union and other groups could have no useful function in modern Indian life. On the contrary, there is still a dearth of student-serving agencies, and many students suffer from a lack of direction. A number of surveys have indicated that the liberalism which was a hallmark of the Indian student community has given way to more conservative attitudes with regard to marriage and family.[12] Furthermore, while a whole generation of Muslim leaders emerged from the ranks of the Muslim Students' Union, the present lack of student groups seems to be creating something of a leadership vacuum.

The Muslim Students' Union is something of an anomaly among student organizations. Because of its communal base, it was able to attract students on the basis of factors related to ideology, particularly during the period of its cooperation with the Muslim League. Yet, the M.S.U. almost never took part in societal political issues and only occassionally in student oriented concerns. It was able, nevertheless, to maintain substantial loyalty from its members, and to build up effective leadership for almost thirty years.

It is difficult to gauge the influence that the Muslim student

[12] Sirsikar, *op. cit.*, p. 7.

organizations have had on the broader Muslim society in Bombay. The alumni of the movement who have been queried on this topic have almost all acknowledged their debt to the organizations. Virtually all of the Muslims in high positions in Bombay's economic, intellectual, and governmental life were in the Muslim student movement. The advocacy of better status for women by the Muslim Students' Union, its propaganda for higher education, and social service work, all contributed to a modernization of the Muslim community.

One of the results of the disappearance of the communal student groups may be an "Indianization" of the student movement. Members of minority groups are in fact taking part in the activities of their local colleges, and are perhaps becoming more cosmopolitan in this way. Social contacts may be expanding, since students are together in groups rather than closed organizations. On the other hand, adjustment to college life may be more difficult without the communal group to act as a cushion.

CHAPTER IX

THE STUDENT PRESS IN INDIA (1930-1965)

THE PRESS has been both a catalyst to and a reflection of social movements in India. Exiled leftists made substantial efforts to smuggle newspapers into India from abroad, feeling that this propaganda campaign was necessary and valuable. Later, the nationalist press in cities like Calcutta and Bombay helped to stimulate the movement and to give it direction. Gandhi's own journal, *Young India*, was influential in the nationalist movement and was one of the main organs of Gandhian philosophy as well as of nationalist propaganda during the 1920s and 1930s. The British authorities recognized the importance of the press by banning newspapers and journals during times of crisis.

A number of generalizations can be made about the student press. It has traditionally been ill-financed and irregular in publication. Much has depended on the dedication of an editor or a small group, which has usually had almost complete autonomy and relative freedom in ideological matters. Most student journals have been published in English, the only medium which could provide a means of communication in a linguistically divided nation. The student press, until very recently, has been an ideological press. The journals which existed were organs of one or another student group. In the very recent period, attempts have been made to start student journals as commercial ventures which serve the student community. Another development in student journalism in India is the rise of the "official" student magazine. In Bombay, most colleges sponsor an annual or semi-annual magazine featuring reports of student activities as well as literary and cultural articles. These journals are edited by students, although they are heavily subsidized by and often strictly controlled by the college administrations. They steer away from political or controversial topics; however, they do provide an outlet for student creative writing.

The circulation of student journals has always been relatively small, averaging 5,000 and seldom exceeding 20,000 for a single journal, even in the heat of the Independence struggle. Despite doubts cast on the effectiveness of the student press, the fact remains that the student organizations devoted a substantial part of their organizational skill and scarce funds to publications.

The Nationalist Student Press

The student press has been a fairly reliable indicator of the overall condition of the student movement. The first politically important magazine was founded around 1930. Prior to this time, *The Students' Brotherhood Quarterly* was published regularly as early as 1912. This journal was strongly influenced by English missionaries. The journal was apparently well financed, for it appeared regularly and was of a high technical quality. Its emphasis was on cultural and educational topics, with occasional student contributions of fiction and poetry. The standards of the editorial work in the journal were high and reflect the elite nature of higher education at this time. Gandhi's own magazine, *Young India*, was also started before 1930, although this journal was not a truly student publication. Many articles in *Young India* were however directed at students, and there is no doubt that many students involved in the nationalist movement received a political education from the journal.

In 1930, one of the first politically oriented student journals appeared in Bombay. The *Young Liberator*, which survived only a short time because of a government ban and inadequate resources, was apparently in the hands of the radicals within the nationalist movement. This journal printed the appeal of the leftist sponsored League Against Imperialism to the Indian National Congress, a document which reflected the views of the left-wing of the Congress and urged the Congress to intensify the 1930 Non-Cooperation Movement. It also printed articles on youth activities in Europe, bringing a consciousness of European student affairs to India for the first time.[1] Although students were involved in distributing clandestine Congress bulletins and propaganda during the 1930s,

---

[1] *Bombay Chronicle*, January 27, 1930, p. 6.

there were no other student publications which had any influence until 1937, when the All-India Students' Federation started a journal which was edited from Bombay.[2]

When the All-India Students' Federation was formed in 1936, it gave the student movement an important impetus. The impetus for the journal came from the leftists within the Students' Federation. This journal, *The Students' Call*, was at first the organ of the B.P.S.F., however, it later achieved national circulation and served as the spokesman of the nationalist student movement.

In their lead editorial, the editors of *The Students' Call* stated :

> A students' magazine is not merely an organ of struggle for students' demands. It is also a training ground where sudents test their intellectual, artistic, and organizational talents and develop them. Viewed from this angle, we in fact wish every school and college in India to have its own magazine or wall-paper for developing the maximum scope for cultural expression on the parts of the students.[3]

The editorial went on to state that the "officially sponsored" magazines did not allow the students sufficient freedom of expression.

One of the greatest problems for the student press in India has been financial. Student organizations have been chronically short of funds. *The Students' Call*, in fact, could not have been published without the financial support of a wealthy nationalist industrialist in Bombay, M. Lotvala, who took an interest in student affairs. Throughout the three years of its existence, *The Students' Call* remained under his patronage.[4] From all indications, financial dependence did not entail any editorial control by adults. The circulation of the journal remained constant at about 2,000, and a total of 30 issues of the magazines were published. It was finally closed owing to a combination of a substantial debt and a government ban on all nationalist publications. Had the government not in-

---

[2] Interview with Dr. Usha Mehta, *loc. cit.*
[3] *The Students' Call*, April, 1937, p. 5.
[4] Interview with Pohekar, *loc cit.*

tervened to suppress the journal in 1940, it would have collapsed under its financial burden.[5] *The Students' Call*, which was judged one of the five best student magazines in the world at an exhibition in New York, never paid its way.[6]

The Students' Call had to maintain a rather delicate balance on its editorial board, since Gandhian nationalists, socialists, and Communists were all actively involved in the publication of the journal. The editorial content of the magazine reflected the leftist views, of its editors, and the journal helped to continue the left-wing trend in the Bombay student movement. *The Call* consistently urged the Congress and the rest of the nationalist movement to take a more radical stance on major national and international issues.

The Call was a well edited magazine, all the more remarkable in a country which had no long journalistic tradition. Political articles constituted the bulk of the material in the magazine, although there were many literary, cultural and scientific items as well. Although *The Students' Call* was never the official organ of the All-India Students' Federation, it exercised a substantial influence on the student movement throughout India. This fact is another indication of the influence of the Bombay student movement on the broader movement in India. *The Call* continued to publish regularly and with an expanded influence and a larger circulation until 1940, when the government banned all student publications during the first nationalist agitation following the outbreak of the Second World War. The students managed to defy the ban by renaming the journal *The Students' Federation*. The journal managed to function until the 1942 movement, which brought strict government control and consorship.[7]

The Students' Call was not the only student publication in India at this time, although it was the largest and most influential. *The Students' Tribune* was founded in 1936 and published for several years by local Students' Federation activists in Lahore and was the official organ of the A.I.S.F. for some time.[8] *The Tribune* was quite similar to *The Call* in its

[5] *Ibid.*
[6] *Blitz*, February 7, 1942, p. 8.
[7] Sakrikar, "History of the Student Movement in India", *op. cit.*, p. 57.
[8] *Ibid.*, p. 45.

coverage and editorial content, although its circulation was somewhat smaller. Both journals cooperated, and there was little overlap of readership. By 1939, there was a flood of student publications. Journals like *The Student, Student Front, Student Review,* and *Collegian Yuvak* (youth) sprang up in various parts of India and were published for a short period of time. Most of these journals, which came from student centers like Calcutta, Madras, Delhi, and several smaller cities, were also relatively radical. The majority of these journals had very small circulations, usually less than 1,000, and many were mimeographed rather than printed. Although most were published in English, a few were issued in regional languages. When faced with the reality of running a magazine on a permanent basis, financial difficulties as well as political problems soon brought these efforts to a halt.

The 1942 movement brought student journalism in Bombay to a temporary standstill, since most nationalist publications were suspended by the British during the height of the struggle. During 1942, however, the students were instrumental in publishing a small mimeographed newspaper, called the *Patrika,* of three or four pages per issue. This journal was published by five or six students, and represented the views of the mainstream of the nationalist student movement. This journal, which was issued weekly by students at Wilson and Ruia Colleges in Bombay, featured propaganda from Congress leaders and articles about various nationalist activities which were otherwise censored by the British. The journal was illegal, and the students had great difficulty in publishing it.[9]

When the 1942 struggle had abated, the British withdrew their ban on nationalist publications, and the student movement once again came out into the open. When the nationalist student press began functioning again its organ was a small journal called *Hind-Praja,* which was turned over to the student movement when it was impossible to start new publications owing to the inability to obtain a paper license. *Hind-Praja* was published biweekly in both Gujarati and English, although most of the student-oriented news was in English.

By any standards, *Hind-Praja* was a sophisticated and well

---

[9] Interview with Pandit, *loc. cit.*

edited student journal. It featured a range of articles, emphasizing political commentary and news of the student movement. Although edited and published in Bombay, *Hind-Praja* had a national circulation, and was read by student groups in all parts of India. Articles such as "The Philosophic Basis of Marxist Communism", "The Real Causes of the Bengal Famine", and long analyses of international events appeared in almost every issue. Prominent leftist leaders such as Ashoka Mehta, Rohit Dave, and Jayaprakash Narayan contributed long articles to the journal, as well as articles from students on a wide range of issues.

Like most student journals, *Hind-Praja* died a death of penury and government repression. Its main problems were financial deficits and an inability or failure to train new staff members. The nationalist student movement felt the loss of its press, and in 1945 the Bombay Students' Congress moved to create a new journal. Since paper restrictions were still in effect, it was necessary for the students to find another sympathetic adult to turn over an already existing journal. A small Gujarati magazine, *Sathi* (Comrade) was turned over to the students and became the organ of the nationalist student movement for more than a year. This journal continued very much in the tradition of its predecessor, *Hind-Praja*, in providing the student movement with a high quality of discussion on political and other matters, and news of the student movement throughout India.[10]

By 1947, however, the nationalist student movement was unable to sustain a publication, and the circulation of *Sathi* had dropped seriously owing to the growing apathy in the student community. Thus, after a number of years of fairly regular publication of various journals, the nationalist student press collapsed along with the rest of the student movement.

The Communist Student Press

A parallel stream in the student press in India are the Communist journals. While magazines like *Hind-Praja* and *Sathi* were espousing the nationalist cause, the Communist

---
[10] Interview with Rohit Dave, former student leader and leading Bombay socialist, January 27, 1965.

dominated All-India Students' Federation was actively promoting its own publications. The student press was one united stream until the split in the student movement which took place in 1940. Thereafter, the organ of the A.I.S.F. remained in the hands of the Communists. The Communists had the advantage of operating a journal with traditions behind it, one which had a substantial fund of loyalty in the student community.

The publication of *The Student* was fairly regular during the period prior to Independence, and it is clear that the Communists did a much more effective job than did the nationalists or socialists in publishing a journal during this period. With funds, printing facilities and occassionally editorial assistance from the Communist Party, the All-India Students' Federation was able to issue a well edited magazine.

The press played a more important role in the Communist student movement than it did among the nationalists. Indeed, in a movement which depended to a large extent on centralized direction, the articles on theoretical and political matters which were printed in *The Student* assumed a substantial importance in the life of the movement. The editorial board of the journal was no amalgam of diverse elements, but was made up of loyal and sophisticated Communists who consciously used the journal as an instrument in the struggle for control of the student movement and for the advancement of Communism in India.[11] Estimates of the circulation of *The Student* very greatly, and range from 3,000 to 15,000. It is probable that the true figure was around 7,000 for most of its existence, reaching a peak around 1947.

The political tone of *The Student* closely followed the guidelines of the Communist Party. The journal was used on many occasions to inform Communist students of changes in the Party's position. During the 1942 struggle, *The Student* strongly supported the "People's War" line, attacking the saboteurs, and even urging students to inform authorities if sabotage was being planned by other students. Later, when the Communists came out in favor of Pakistan, *The Student* acti-

[11] Interview with Munesh Saxena, former editor of *The Student*, March 3, 1965.

vely courted the communal Muslim elements, while only a few months before it had viciously attacked these very elements. The journal was much interested in student unity, and its pages were filled with calls for unity. It was, naturally, quite violently opposed to the nationalist student organizations, and particularly to the socialists, whom they called anti-democratic elements.

Although the main thrust of the content was political, *The Student* was a well-balanced journal. Its coverage of science was as good as any journal in India at the time, and occasionally fiction and poetry were found on its pages as well as sports news. All through its existence, the journal was quite interested in international affairs, although almost always from the Communist point of view. The only reason that *The Student* did not wield more influence than it actually did was because of its almost total dependence on the Communist Party for ideological guidance, causing the journal to take unpopular stands on many issues of the day.

The Student published more or less continuously from 1941 until 1953, with a slight interruption during the Ranadive period in 1948 because of a brief government ban on Communists publications. This is a remarkable achievement for an Indian student journal, and it was, in fact, the longest period of more or less continuous publication in the history of Indian student journalism. During most of its history, *The Student* was published from Bombay. Only during its final period were a number of moves made when the journal followed its editor from Calcutta to Madras, and later to Delhi.

Student Journalism in Post-Independence India

The "golden age" of student journalism in India ended with Independence in 1947. Like the rest of the student movement, the student press suffered an eclipse. The causes for the decline are not hard to find. When a large part of the constituency of the student movement disappeared in 1947, many students who previously supported the student press were no longer interested in it. Moreover, financial and moral support, which had come from elements of the adult movements, ceased and the friendly attitude of the adult parties changed into apathy or overt hostility.[12]

Thus, by 1949, there was almost a vacuum in the area of student publications. Since Independence, there have been several attempts to revive the student press in India, and there are a handful of journals presently in existence. During the immediate post-Independence period, several adult publications tried to cater to the student community and achieved a small amount of influence for a short period. *Blitz*, a left-wing weekly published in Bombay, featured a regular student column for a while, and *Forum* magazine, also from Bombay, printed regular articles concerning student affairs.

One of the first student organizations to make an attempt to revive student journalism after Independence was the National Union of Students. During the decade between 1950 and 1960, it made a number of attempts to operate student magazines. However, because of financial difficulties, or simple inefficiency, these journals collapsed quickly. A magazine called *University News* was issued in 1953. Under the sponsorship of the National Union of Students, this journal featured news of the student movement and a number of articles on the educational system and proposed reform measures. It kept rather strictly away from partizan political issues, although it was often critical of the educational policies of the Congress government.

In the period since 1955, there have been a number of attempts to establish journals to meet the needs of the student community. One of the earliest of these attempts was a magazine entitled *Young India* (after Gandhi's journal of the same name), which was published from Delhi by a group of former students. This publication, which was issued rather irregularly owing to lack of funds, was intended to be an all-India student journal serving the student community with news and comments on student activities. However, the journal's circulation is effectively limited to the Delhi area and it has never been influential in the student community, even in Delhi. Although the magazine is still in existence, it is now published very irregularly, and its circulation is well under 5,000.

A similar venture is *The Student's Digest*, a journal published from Bombay. This magazine has a circulation of about

[12] Interview with Sakrikar, *loc. cit.*

7,000 and has been issued fairly regularly for seven years. Although *The Digest* has been successful in attracting advertizers, its articles are uninteresting and unrelated to the needs and concerns of the student community. Like *Young India*, the editors of *The Students' Digest* have moved further from the mainstream of the student community, and the journal now confines itself to reprinting articles from other magazines and from foreign governments.

In the past several years, the National Council of University Students of India has attempted to publish a magazine for Indian students. This journal, called *The Students' Chronicle*, has come out intermittently for the past few years, and has been somewhat better edited than most student publications. Its emphasis, however, has been on international student affairs, which are of little interest to the average Indian student and it has generally followed the lead of the government educationists on matters of policy. The magazine has not been particularly popular, and it suffers from both financial and staff difficulties. Another publication sponsored by the National Student Press Council of India, *Indian Student News*, has been somewhat more successful. (This Press Council is an off shoot of the N.C.U.S.I.). A weekly newsletter is issued by the N.S.P.C.I. which covers events of importance to students, concentrating on matters of student politics and official educational issues. Both the N.C.U.S.I. and the N.S.P.C.I. are dependent on outside financial support for their continued existence.

In addition to these private ventures, several "official" youth magazines have appeared in the past decade. The most important of these was the *Youth Congress*, the organ of the All-India Youth Congress. This publication was issued regularly each month up to September, 1965, when the Youth Congress was dissolved by the adult Congress organization. *Youth Congress* was atmost a complete failure. Despite a very substantial subsidy for publication, the journal achieved no impact whatsoever on the student community, and its circulation seemed to have been limited to functionaries of the Congress organization and the Youth Congress. One of the main reasons for its failure, of course, was the nature of the Youth Congress itself, which was not a viable student or youth movement, but rather a club for aspiring young politicians. The content of

Youth Congress was generally concerned with news of the activity of the Youth Congress, along with speeches, articles, and pictures of Congress leaders.

The Ministry of Education has published a magazine for youth during the past several years. The journal, entitled *Youth*, stresses the Five-Year Plans and has given much attention to the National Discipline Scheme. It is free from political commentary, although it has supported various government educational and development schemes. The journal, which is printed on expensive paper, and is handsomely edited, is not written by students or young people and is read by very few of them.

Student political groups have also tried to issue journals during the period since 1947. The Communist student organizations have been the most successful in their efforts, since they have had the fairly consistent financial and organizational support of the Communist Party. In recent years, however, their publications program has been serioulsy disoriented by the split within the Communist movement. The adult party, fearing that the organs of the student movement would become favorable to the leftist "pro-Chinese" grouping within the movement, stopped all publications for a period, and have only recently began to allow the youth and student fronts of the Communists to issue a small publication called *New Generation*. This monthly journal, which has come out for several years, has not attracted much attention in the student community and has printed articles on both political and educational topics.

Almost every college in Bombay issues an annual or semi-annual college magazine. These publications, which have been mentioned earlier, are now the mainstay of Indian student journalism. They are heavily subsidized and controlled by the colleges, and the circulation of the magazines is usually limited to the colleges in which they are published. In most colleges, sections in English are included in addition to articles in various Indian languages. In some of the larger colleges, there are articles in such Indian languages as Tamil, Urdu, Hindi, Gujarati, Marathi, or Bengali, in addition to a large English section. Students who are literate but not fluent in English thereby have an opportunity to make a contribution to the magazine in their mother tongue. Indeed, the regional language sections are often more imaginative than the English section.

Articles on a wide range of subjects are found in these publications, although care is taken to avoid particularly controversial or political topics. Poetry, some of it of high quality, is included, as are short stories, and other pieces of fiction. The bulk of the writing, however, is taken up by short essays on a variety of topics, ranging from international affairs to agriculture. Book reviews are also common, as are short sections describing the activities of the various extra-curricular groups of the college.

Conclusion

There is a sharp contrast between the student press in the pre-Independence and post-Independence periods. Prior to 1947, student magazines served an important function: they provided the medium of communication for an active movement and gave the political leadership of the movement a means for propaganda and political education. While the journals of the student organizations had little impact or the majority of the student population, even during the Independence struggle, they did help to provide continuity and stability to a movement. The post-1947 period has seen a sharp decline in both the quality and quantity of student journalism in Bombay. The main reason for this is the decline in the overall student movement and the virtual disappearance of student organizations devoted to politics. The decline of the student press has, however, taken away a means of communications from the students which might be valuable even in the current period.

Chapter X

THE TRANSITION OF THE BOMBAY STUDENT MOVEMENT

THIS FINAL chapter has two fundamental purposes, which are aimed at placing the study in its proper prespective and at distilling some general trends from a mass of material concerning students, politics, and higher education in Bombay. After summarizing the findings of the descriptive section of the study, an effort will be made to delineate some of the recurring patterns. Student activity in Bombay has been the product mainly of external factors. Politically, the student movement would not have grown without the impetus of the nationalist struggle of the 1920s and 1930s. The strong student organizations which influenced the campus during this period were largely dependent on their environment for impetus. Student cultural activity, while more spontaneous, has also been substantially influenced by the attitudes of university administrators, the general public, and other educational factors. The patterns of student activity—of the rise and fall of militant student groups and their public support—vary with changing societal non-student factors. This does not mean that university students have been unable to accomplish anything in the area of extra-curricular activities. On the contrary, students were instrumental in the cultural renaissance of Bengal in the early part of the twentieth century, and were an important element in nationalist cultural and political activity later in the century. Yet, the fact that the student movement almost collapsed when the nationalist political struggle ended, and the attitude of educational and political leaders changed is an indication of the dependence of the movement on outside factors.

The fact that student political activity has been so dependent on outside factors raises the question as to whether there has been a true student movement in Bombay, and in India generally. If by movement we mean a well organized definable group with specific aims, consciously functioning publicly in support of its aims, then there has been a student movement in Bombay. It is true that the movement has been sporadic, often ill-organized, and divided by differences in ideologies and interests. Yet, the students have played a conscious political role on a number of occasions during the past half-century, and their organized efforts in political and other spheres have been important to the development of higher education in India, as well as to political events.

Summary of the Findings

This summary can hope to provide but a glimpse of an eventful, formative period in the development of student activities and politics in Bombay, spanning nearly half a century. This section is intended to indicate some of the salient factors which have shaped student politics and general activities. Characteristics of student activity which have been observed in Bombay may or may not be relevant to other countries in other historical periods. It is hoped, however, that this analytical framework will provide the basis for further consideration of student activity in differing circumstances.

Student Politics and National Events

One of the major changes in the student movement has come with the divorce of student politics from national politics in India. The political parties, with the partial exception of the Communists, have withdrawn their support from the campuses. They have been relatively sincere in their protestations that politics should be divorced from the colleges and universities. During the Independence struggle, the political parties actively sought student support and considered the students as valuable allies in their political and ideological campaigns. Politics in India has lost much of its altruistic glitter and ideological purity in the struggle to function in an independent nation, thus causing many idealistic students to eschew the seeming rampant corruption of the broader political parties. It can truthfully be stated that while at one time students played an active and at times important part in the broader political arena of Bombay, they no longer take a direct interest in politics. Some of the causes for lack of student interest in politics have been previously discussed. Academic issues and grievances relating directly to inadequate academic programs, economic insecurity, or bad living conditions have not motivated the students in the direction of sustained unrest or political action.

The major trends in student politics in Bombay are not difficult to discern in the light of the material presented in this study. The campus, since 1947, has witnessed a rapid apoliticalization; today there is scarcely a single student political organization actively functioning, to say nothing of a movement. In contrast to the broader society, where politics remains a major concern of the literate population, albeit without its image of idealism and ideology, the student world seems to have renounced politics altogether. However, student attitude surveys in Bombay and Poona show that only a small minority of the present generation of students is involved in politics; the interviews and other material presented in this study corroborate this finding. Thus, the pre-Independence trend was in the direction of student involvement in national issues and a substantial political awareness on the campus; the more recent period has been a reversal of this trend.

Organizational Characteristics of Student Movements and Groups

Student organizations, especially those without "official" patronage and support, tend to be unstable and short-lived. In Bombay, mass student movements were usually based on rather specific political or academic issues, and lasted only as long as these issues remained vividly imprinted in the consciousness of the student population. Even the nationalist student movement, which was able to maintain itself for a number of years, suffered from the ebbs and flows of Gandhi's various campaigns. The movement all but disappeared during periods of political calm, despite the determined efforts of sophisticated student leaders.

The causes for this instability are not difficult to find. The student population is itself quite unstable; a student "generation" lasts three or four years at most. Furthermore, many student activists have brief attention spans; they withdraw from a particular cause or organization relatively quickly, retreating into the coffee houses and taking to the streets to protest at irregular intervals. Student groups are also subject to the vagaries of academic life and the restrictions of academic examination schedules, as well as to changes in political climate. Even organizations unrelated to politics show a good deal of instability, although such "special interest" groups lead a more independent existence.

Among the politically oriented organizations, value-oriented groups are better able to withstand organizational instability than those based on specific issues or short-term causes. The ideological commitment of at least a portion of the membership of such organizations provides a stabilizing force. Value-oriented groups use specific issues for broader purposes and are able to fall back on their commitment to a particular ideology or set of beliefs when a campaign has ended. Norm-oriented student organizations, of a political or non-political nature, are oriented towards specific issues which, when settled or clearly defeated, leaves the group without a *raison d'etre*.

Norm-oriented groups concern themselves with specific issues, not seeking basic changes in the social, political, or educational system, while value-oriented organizations have a broader ideology which allows them to contribute to and frequently exploit many issues and circumstances during periods of political consciousness. Norm-oriented groups live from crisis to crisis and often steer away from tight organizational structures or restrictive statements of purpose in favor of amorphousness. While this may assure the involvement of large numbers of students over a specific issue, it paralyzes the organization when the impetus must come from internal, imaginative leadership in the absence of an external crisis. For the most part, only when movements are value-oriented (as in specific campaigns of the nationalist movement or in the "matriculation massacre" of 1936) can they be sustained when the specific focus is changed.

There are a number of important differences between the political student groups which have received most attention in this study, and other organizations devoted to educational, cultural, or social activity. The focus of the non-political groups naturally means that they will be under less pressure from outside forces. Furthermore, such groups naturally have long-range interests, and are organized with a view toward continued survival. Since they do not constitute a threat to governmental or educational authorities they often have the tacit or active cooperation of university administrators. The uncontroversial nature of most non-political student activity involves less commitment from members than does a value-oriented political struggle; the activity of such non-political organizations is less intense, although generally more stable. Although both political and non-political student groups are similar in some of their characteristics, they do exhibit major differences as well.

The Life Cycles of Student Movements

It is clear that not all student organizations are movements, although organizations can build movements. However, many student groups which aspire to become movements or which call themselves "movements" cannot truthfully be defined as such. Student discussion groups have been known to change the opinions of their members, while larger movements of students have had a direct impact on society.

A student movement can be generated in a number of ways. It can arise spontaneously from a deeply felt need of large numbers of students. It can arise from specific agitational campaigns, or it can be consciously created by a cadre of students seeking, for reasons of political ideology or civic responsibility, to launch a movement for a specific goal. Nevertheless, if the particular issue is not relevant to the student population, the movement, whatever its source, will be a failure. The attempt to create a movement to support the ideas of Moral Re-Armament, although lavishly financed and well led, failed for want of interest among students.

Student movements in Bombay have tended to be rather non-ideological in their approach to issues and events. Even those movements led by politically sophisticated, even sectarian, students have stressed issues and not ideologies. The 1942 struggle is an example of this tendency. This movement, which had the support of the large majority of the students in Bombay and which succeeded in closing the city's colleges for several months, stressed a very simple program — support for the "Quit India" slogan and protest against the arrest of Gandhi and the other Congress leaders. Although most of the important leaders of the campaign were sophisticated socialist students, broader matters of ideology had little impact on the students and the leadership was unsuccessful in "politicizing" the struggle. Similarly, although the morning college agitation has aroused some concern among Bombay's students, the Communist-oriented Bombay Students' Union failed in its attempt to turn the agitation into a political movement.

A student movement, which necessarily involves a mass upsurge of student interest and activity (although not necessarily of agitation) may be guided by formal organizational structures, or it may be entirely spontaneous and organizationally amorphous. On the one hand, it is possible for a movement to create a continuing organization by institutionalizing itself. On the other, it is also possible for a movement which ends in failure (or, for that matter, in total victory) to destroy any organizations which were involved in it. Thus, in differing circumstances, movements can create organizations, and organizations can also stimulate movements.

While much of the attention of this study has been devoted to movements, and, while these phenomena are the most dramatic manifestations of student activity, the less volatile organizations are also of primary importance. Smaller groups and societies have often played a key role in shaping the student population, and have been instrumental in stimulating broader movements.

Students and Politics

Two distinctions may be made when considering the political interests of the student movement in Bombay. The first distinction concerns the contrast between the highly ideological but very small minority of cadres and the mass of more pragmatic student participants. Even at the apex of any student movement, a group, numbering perhaps five hundred at most, was concerned with the ideological distinctions of the various political organizations, a small cadre in a movement involving tens of thousands. The second important distinction which must be made concerning student politics and ideology has been implied earlier in this study. The period following 1947 has seen a decline of ideology in the student movement and in Indian political life. Again, the student movement has reflected the changes in society.

Most observers of the student scene in Bombay have noted that left-wing student groups made lasting impact on the thinking of students of the pre-Independence generation. This fact may have contributed to the present day prevalence of left-wing jargon which characterizes Indian politics. The interviews held with several hundred past and present student leaders have given unmistakable evidence that politics has been important at least to the elite segment of the studen population.

Student Leadership and Political Involvement

During the Independence struggle, much of the politically active student leadership came almost exclusively from the upper and middle classes and from students with very high academic and social standings within their colleges. While exact figures are unavailable, interviews with educators and former student leaders provide sufficient indications concerning the nature of student leadership in Bombay. At this period, participation in student politics was considered prestigious, and most of those student leaders who went to jail during the various struggles came from wealthy backgrounds. Since 1947, the situation has changed markedly. Students from the upper classes and upper academic levels, in both the natural sciences and liberal arts, shun student politics. While many of the more alert students have an intellectual interest in national and world politics, they almost invariably refrain from participation in any of the student political organizations. Much of the leadership has been taken over by students from the lower middle classes, who have some experience with education and a reasonably good command of English, but who are unfortunately less well prepared than upper class students. Participation in student politics is no longer a mark of academic distinction; if anything, it has become the opposite. Students from the lower classes, who are clearly the most oppressed individuals in the higher educational system, take only a small part in the existing student organizations and do not generally participate in movements, even when they involve issues of direct concern to them, such as the morning college question. Such students seem to be too much concerned with their academic careers to risk political activity. Furthermore, their unfamiliarity with the system of higher education and with the English language, in which their colleges are conducted, form an almost insurmountable barrier to political activity.

The Function of the Student Movement in Society and Politics

With the exception of the 1942 struggle, the direct impact of students on society in Bombay has been minimal. Students have on occasion aroused political protest among the public on particular issues, but they have usually failed to institute any changes. Particularly in contrast to the mass student movements of Japan, Korea and other nations, the Indian student movement appears singularly ineffective.

Student organizations have tried, usually in vain, to influence educational decisions. It is important to note that such attempts have almost always dealt with specific issues of direct urgency to the students themselves, such as examinations or fee increases, and not with broader issues of educational policy. Yet, despite this general student refusal to take an active interest in the important issues concerning Indian higher education, there have been some rewarding results of student agitations. Reappraisal of the examination system, fee structure, and other specific reforms have been instituted as a direct result of student agitation, as well as the correcting of much more minor inequities in the system.

It is clear that with only a few exceptions students have played only a peripheral role in the broader society. They were at no time in the vanguard of the independence movement, although their support for leftists within the movement was at that time important. The reasons for the relative unimportance of the students are connected with the overall strength of the nationalist movement, which had a developed leadership and did not need to rely on the students, and to Indian intellectual life at the time, which was able to provide trained and ideologically sophisticated leadership.

The Role of Student Organizations on the Campus

Until now, this summary has dealt rather broadly with the role of the student movement as a whole and with its political segment in particular, concerning its role in modern Indian

society. It is also necessary to look more closely at the student
organizations themselves, since these groups constitute the
keystone of any movement and are the ongoing manifestations
of student interest in a variety of issues.

In this summary, much has already been said about the
function of political student organizations in the student movement and on the campus. Although without support from the
colleges or universities, many of the more established student
political groups have been quite long-lived. The vetaran
Communist student organization, for example, has had a continued existence since 1940, and the socialist groups have also
had a long, although somewhat less stable, existence. As has
been noted, the activity of the various political student organizations has varied greatly in different periods. During times
of political awareness in the city as a whole, the political student
groups were able to attract large numbers of students to meetings and other activities. When, however, broader political
issues were not in the public eye, the activity of the student
groups was on a much lower level. The impact of the broader
political parties on the student groups has already been noted.

Of much more importance during the post-1947 period have
been the non-political organizations. Cultural and Social
student organizations have had a long history in Bombay and
have maintained a consistently high level of activity through
the years. While the college authorities have given much more
support to such groups in recent years than the past, they have
always had at least the tacit approval of educators and administrators.

There are a wide variety of non-political student groups
which have been active in Bombay, and it is not possible to
discuss them all in detail here. It may be valuable, however,
to list some of the more important types of groups : (1) cultural
groups—such organizations as English Literary Societies,
dramatic groups, both English and vernacular, dance groups,
vernacular literary groups; (2) social groups—these usually
include regional student associations which have mainly social
goals; (3) religious groups—most religious minorities, such as
the Parsis, Sikhs, Muslims, have strong associations among the
students; (4) sports groups—these are usually directly sponsored by the colleges and exist for both men and women; (5)

student unions and publishing committees—most colleges have a student union, elected by the students with the strict supervision of the college administration, on a generally non-political basis. These unions occassionally concern themselves with matters of politics, but are usually confined to supervision of officially sponsored student activities. The student committees which publish the college magazines and journals are also a source of extra-curricular activity. In addition to these well-defined groups, there exist many informal student groups. Such groups, which often meet for discussion or informal social purposes, may have an impact on student attitudes and patterns of socialization and have occassionally been of great importance to both political and social organizations.

In the foregoing sections of this study, the socializing role of the ethnic and religious student groups has been discussed. The debating and publication groups have given politically inclined students training in aspects of political processes and techniques. The literary societies have improved standards of English or have fostered scholarly study of the vernacular languages.

As a means of socialization, particularly for the financially poorer students, the social and cultural associations have been more effective than have the political groups. Within admittedly rigid limits, these organizations are usually free to plan programs that are of interest to the students. Students often see participation in such groups as a means of upward mobility in college, or as valuable training for a later career. It is true that the training gained in non-political student groups has provided a firm basis for careers in law, politics, drama, music, and other activities. Thus, it is unwise to underestimate the importance of the mundane non-political student groups on both politics and other aspects of life. This is particularly true in the recent period, which has been marked by a decline in politics on the campuses.

Student organizations have had a varied impact on the student population over the years. Students who are vocationally oriented have not found the extra-curricular student activities appealing, and the percentages of students participating in such activities has varied over the years. However, throughout the years there has always been the dependable minority

who always participates in these activities regardless of
the state of affairs. Yet, in spite of their undramatic nature,
these quiet non-political groups have provided a means of
acclimatization to college or urban life and have given a sense
of greater self-confidence to students with little experience
of higher education. Groups have provided training in various areas, as well as conditions under which student and
teacher might meet in an unrestrained setting. The intellectual
activity carried on in student organizations has for some
students supplemented and sometimes taken the place of the
more formal offerings of the college curriculum.

Hypotheses Suggested by the Study

The present study has presented a broad range of empircal
material concerning the history and development of the student
movement in Bombay. In the introductory chapter, a number of
hypotheses concerning student activity in general were suggested. In the light of the material presented in this study, it is
possible to present some hypotheses to see if they are applicable to the data and possibly to suggest their broader relevance.

The hypothesis that extremist views often stimulate greater
commitment in an organization from the leadership and the
rank and file is reflected in this study. This greater commitment appears to enhance directly the vigor of an organization.
It is clear that the extreme left and right-wing student groups
in Bombay have survived many shifts in political climate and
have maintained full programs. Both the Communist-dominated Bombay Students' Union and the right-wing R.S.S. and
Vidyarthi Parishad have been consistently more active than
other groups. In retrospect, moreover, the left-wing leadership
of the nationalist student movement during the Independence
struggle, sustained by a broader socialist ideology, was the
primary force in the leadership of the student movement. The
notable failure of the Congress and other moderate parties to
attract continuous student support is another indication of
the relationship of ideological commitment and the condition
of an organization.

It has been hypothesized that student leadership comes from
fairly definable groups within the student population. In

Bombay, the study has suggested that this is at least partly true, for most of the leaders of political organizations, at least before 1947, came from upper classes and castes but that there was little distinction between regional groups. One of the main causes for the sudden withdrawal of upper class students from political involvement is the contamination of politics by widespread corruption. Politics is no longer ranked in the highly prestigious bracket of professions such as medicine and engineering; the natural sciences have displaced politics. There has been a marked influx of upper class students into the natural sciences. This is understandable both because the natural sciences are often the most vital and rewarding (intellectually, socially and, later, financially) fields in modern India and also because upper class students, by virtue of their better academic preparation, are more able to meet the stiff requirements of the natural sciences. In the course of this study it has become apparent that science students were conspicuous in their lack of political involvement. Furthermore, students of the natural sciences regard their college year as indispensable preparation for their professional careers. Correspondingly, they are more single-minded and loathe to risk their prospects through student indiscipline or political involvement. Students in the liberal arts, on the other hand, risk less, in view of their indifferent career prospects, by becoming political activists; moreover, they are more disposed to question societal problems.[1] In view of all his evidence, it is astonishing that there has not been far more serious and intense student indiscipline from large segments of the student population.

One of the key hypotheses in this study has concerned the pattern of student political life and its relationship to the broader society. The pattern of student life in Bombay has been one of rhythmic alternation between growth and decline of fairly strong student movements. The causes for the rise of the student movement in Bombay are not difficult to discern. The political fermentation which took place during the nationalist struggle provided a powerful impetus to aware young people,

---

[1] See Spencer, *op. cit.*, and Soares, op. cit., for a more detailed discussion of this important factor.

and the politics of the nationalist organizations soon spread to the campus.

The basis of politics in India has changed. This transformation has proved to be a far less fertile ground for the development of a student political movement. Political awareness remains high among India's literate minority, but the idealistic struggles of the nationalist movement have replaced by the day to day compromises of a firmly entrenched Congress Party. The opposition both left and right, is so far from power that their appeal is reduced and their pronouncements taken without much seriousness. The growth of regional and interest groups politics has further altered the basis of Indian politics. All these changes may well be necessary in view of the reality of Indian policy, but they are not conducive to a large and politically active student movement. Students are less willing than their elders to tolerate compromise, demanding a moral or ideological crusade for which to fight.

These are some of the reasons for the decline in the student political movement in Bombay and in India generally. The problems and perplexities of modern India will not lend themselves to quick and conclusive solutions; and as long as conditions remain unchanged, it is unlikely that in the foreseeable future a strong student movement will emerge in modern India. Even a strong government effort to arouse student concern and interest during the Chinese invasion of 1962 failed to evoke much student response. Many students feared that they were being exploited by the Congress politicians, and their fear and distrust of the politicians overcome their patriotic motivation.

The lack of a continuing student movement in India does not mean that there will be no more indiscipline. On the contrary, trends in Indian higher education indicate that the decline of quality and increasing pressure to expand enrollments in the face of limited resources will continue unabated for some time, and that the crucial language problem in higher education will become more acute and widespread as demands for the use of the vernacular languages become more vociferous. There would seem to be no end to the kind of sporadic agitation which was seen recently during the Madras language riots (when more than thirty were killed and millions of dollars of damage was done in an agitational campaign directed and carried out primarily by students with the support of opposition political leaders) or during the campaign to bring down the government of the state or Orissa. In this latter instance, the students, again with the support of opposition politicians, sought to focus attention on alleged corruption by the state Chief Minister, and succeeded in forcing an investigation in which their charges proved correct, and the minister involved resigned, causing considerable embarrassment to the Congress government.

These instances of effective, but diffuse, political action by students, which could be multiplied many times, do not indicate the presence of an ongoing student movement. Rather, unrest which does take place is the overflow of resentment which exists below the surface in much of India's student population. That there has not been more agitation in recent years is much more surprising than the rather long catalog of riots and demonstrations which have taken place.

Conclusion

The student organizations and movements considered in this study reflect broader political and educational trends in Bombay and in India, and that the students as a modern group, sensitive to political and social change, are a particularly telling group to study when investigating the nature of modernization and political change in a developing nation. It goes without saying that the students are an important group merely because they are an incipient elite (this is probably less true in India than in the other developing nations). They are also important as an indicator of developments in other segments of society. The disillusionment of the student movement immediately following Independence in India was followed in later years by a gradual de-emphasis of ideology in politics and a tarnishing of the nationalist idealism engendered by the struggle in broader political realm. The student movement has shown the interaction of the all important religious and regional groups in Indian politics. The splits and disagreements which have been documented in this study between the Muslim and Hindu segments of the nationalist movement and the growth of a pro-Pakistan Muslim student movement during the 1940s was also a pattern of the broader political movements in India. The fact that this study has made possible a detailed organizational analysis of this development is significant, and may add to the knowledge of this crucial period in the political history of the Indian subcontinent.

TABLE 1

HISTORICAL DEVELOPMENT OF THE STUDENT POLITICAL MOVEMENT IN BOMBAY AND RELATED EVENTS

1889	Students' Brotherhood formed—moderately radical in views, discussion-oriented
1890	Muslim Students' Union formed—not directly political, although concerned with public issues
1900-1920	Young Men's Hindu Association, Young Men's Parsi Association, and other groups
1920	Gandhi's Non-Cooperation Movement
1920	Hind Vidyarthi Sabha (Indian Students' Organization) formed
1921	Young Collegians—politicaly liberal-oriented discussion group
1925	Rashtriya Swamasevak Sangh founded—strongly Hindu-oriented right-wing, although not directly involved in partizan politics
1930	Bombay Youth League—strongly nationalist and radical, active in Civil Disobedience Movement —Bombay Students' Swadeshi League —Students' Anti-Untouchable League —National Youth League
1930-1934	Gandhi's Civil Disobedience Movement
1934	Congress Socialist Party formed
1936	"Matriculation Massacre," first large scale student demonstration

1936	All-India Students' Federation founded
	—Bombay Presidency Students' Federation
	—Bombay Presidency Students' Federation
	—Bombay Students' Union
	   —North Bombay Students' Union
	   —Bombay Suburban Students' Union
	—strongly nationalist and radical in politics, direct action-oriented

1937	All-India Muslim Students' Federation founded—allied with the communalist Muslim League—Bombay Presidency Muslim Students' League
1937	Sikh Students' Federation founded

1940	All-India Students' Federation splits into two wings — one Gandhian-socialist and the other Communist —Bombay Students' Union and Bombay Presidency Students' Federation also split into two separate organizations, both retaining the same name
1940	Radical Students' Union (Royist) formed
1941	Rashtra Seva Dal founded—socialist-dominated cultural and political association
1942	Mass "Quit India" movement sponsored by the Congress
1943	Students' Unity Committee founded—an attempt to unite the various non-Communist elements in the student movement
1945	All-India Students' Congress founded — supersedes the nationalist segment of the All-India Students' Federation —Bombay Students' Congress incorporates the Unity Committee
1949	All-India Youth Congress founded—under the auspices of the All-India Congress Committee
1950	National Union of Students founded
1953	Samajwadi Yuvak Sabha (socialist youth organization) founded
1955	Vidyarthi Parishad founded—right-wing student organization
1958	All-India University Union Preparatory Committee formed to supersede the National Union of Students
1960	National Council of University Students of India formed to supercede the A.I.U.U.P.C.
1962	National Youth Front formed to resist Chinese aggression

TABLE 2

POLITICAL TENDENCIES IN THE INDIAN STUDENT MOVEMENT
(1900-1965)

Marxist Left	Socialist	Social-Democratic	Moderate	Conservative	Communalist
A.I.S.F. (Communist) (1940-65)	Samajwadi Yuvak Sabha (1953-65)	Students' Brotherhood (1889-1937)		Sikh Students' Federation (1937-49)	Rashtriya Swamasevak Sangh (R.S.S.) (1925-65)
Bombay Youth League (1930)	Students' Unity Committee (1943)	Muslim Students' Union (1890-1965)		Muslim Students' Federation (1937-47)	
					Hindu Students' Federation (1935-55)
Bombay Students' Union (1936-47)	Rashtra Seva Dal (1949-65)	Youth Congress			
Bombay Students' Congress (1945-48)	Radical Students' Union (1940-47)	National Council of University Students (1960-65)			
A.I.S.F. (Nationalist) (1936-49)		National Union of Students (1950-63)			Vidyarthi Parishad (1955-65)
			National Youth Front (1962-64)		

INDEX

Acharya, P. B., 151
Activity, Student, *see* Student Activity
Adil, Adam, 138
adolescence, 3, 5
Africa, 1, 20
Ahluwalia, Sagar, 19, 60, 78, 98
Akhil Bharatiya Vidyarthi Parishad, *see* Vidyarthi Parishad
Aligarh Muslim University, 181
All-India College Students' Conference : Nagpur session 1920, 60-61; Ahmedabad session, 61
All-India Congress Committee, 100, 138
All-India Kisan Sabha, 101
All-India Muslim Students' Federation, 78, 117, 178
All-India Students' Congress, 88, 120-126, 137
All-India Students' Federation, 13, 74, 75, 77, 85-89, 101, 108, 117, 120, 122, 123, 127, 129, 139, 141, 144, 186, 187, 190
All-India Trade Union Congress, 64, 89, 101
Altbach, Philip G., 19, 131
Ambedkar, B. R., 40, 42
America, Latin, 1, 15
Asia, 1
Azad, Maulana Abul Kalam, 122

Bardoli, 68
Batliwala, Soli, 63, 83, 84
Bengal, 57, 58, 71, 118, 120, 129, 196
Bharat Sevak Samaj, 167
Blitz, 192
Bombay, a key commercial city, 23; educational system in, 23-24; University of, 24; size and composition of student population, 25-26; main centre of higher education, 28; primary education in, 29-31; secondary education in, 31-34; higher education in, 35-37, 50-54; colleges in, 37-50; roots of student movement in, 57-72; early student activity, 57-64; Students' Brotherhood, 64-67; Youth League, 67-70; politicization of student movement in, 73-99; educational development and student activity, 89-96; effect of 1942 movement on students, 100-112; students and independence, 1943-47, 113-133; Naval Mutiny, 73, 129-130; student politics since 1947, 134-170; Youth Congress, 137-139; communist student movement in, 139-143; socialist student movement in, 144-148; right-wing student movement in, 148-153; student agitation 1947-65, 153-157; "morning college" question, 157-160; National Union of Students in, 160-164; non-political student activity in, 164-168; student press in, 184-195; transition of student movement in, 196-211
Bombay Chronicle, 63, 68, 75, 76, 77, 80, 87, 91, 92, 94, 95, 98, 105, 111, 119, 120, 124, 125, 138, 141, 144, 154, 155, 156, 178
Bombay Presidency Muslim Students' Federation, 178, 179, 180
Bombay Presidency (Provincial) Students' Federation, 74, 79, 80, 85, 186
Bombay Presidency Students' Conference, 98: 1936 session, 79-80; 1937 session, 81-82; 1938 session, 82
Bombay Provincial Congress Committee (B.P.C.C.), 137, 138
Bombay Provincial Muslim Youth Federation, 179

Bombay Students' Congress, 124-126, 136, 137, 154, 156, 189
Bombay Students' Medical Scheme, 161
Bombay Students' Swadeshi League, 63
Bombay Students' Union (B.S.U.), 44, 64, 74-82, 88, 97, 102, 103, 104, 114, 115, 116, 117, 124, 127, 128, 129, 141, 154, 155, 156, 200, 206; affiliate of the Provincial Federation, 74; three units of, 74; split in, 75, 78; formation of Working Committee, 75-76; democratic functioning of, 76; role in political movements, 76-77; Wilson College strike of 1932, 77; membership, 78, 140; social work, 78-79; 1936 conference, 79-80; 1938 conference, 81; demonstrations against Dwyer, 81-82; and "matriculation massacre", 91; loss of strength since 1947, 139; change in nature of activities, 142-143; on morning colleges, 159
Bombay University, see University of Bombay
Bombay Youth League, 62, 63, 67-70, 71, 77
Bose, Subhas Chandra, 62, 68, 75, 82, 85, 126
Brahmins, 25, 26, 149
British Raj, 74
Burma, 2, 4, 20

Calcutta, 35, 58, 62, 69, 169, 184, 188
Chagla, M. C., 176
Chandra, Prabadh, 63
Chaudhary, N. B., 167
City Students' Action Committee, 140, 159
civil disobedience, 62, 69, 93, 100, 108, 125
co-education, 27
Communist International, 84

Communist Party of India, 13, 58, 66, 85, 88, 89, 101, 128, 129, 139, 140, 141, 142, 143, 190
Communist Student Movement, 63, 66, 67, 83-85, 104, 114, 115, 126-129, 135, 139-143
Communists, 73, 76, 81, 83, 84, 85, 86, 87, 88, 89, 97, 101, 102, 103, 104, 105, 108, 114, 115, 116, 117, 118, 119, 127, 128, 129, 139, 140, 141, 143, 190
Congress Party, see Indian National Congress
Congress Radio, 107-108
Congress Seva Dal, 167
Congress Socialist Party, 73, 76, 82, 84, 144
Congress Volunteer Corps, 79
Cormack, Margaret, 27
Cripps Mission, 100
Curran, J. A., 148

Dalal, Chandrakant, 118, 120
Dandavate, M. R., 126, 166
Dange, S. A., 58, 83, 98
Dastur, Dr. Aloo J., 95
Dave, Rohit, 186
Dengle, Nana, 147
Developing countries, importance of student movements, 1-2; characteristics of students in, 2-6; higher education in, 2; pressures on students in, 6-10
dock explosion, 119
Dongerkery, S. R., 111
Dwyer, Sir Maurice, 81, 121

Eastman, Max, 83
Education, higher, see Higher Education
Education in Bombay: primary, 29-31; secondary, 31-34; higher, 35-37; colleges, 37-50
Elphinstone College, 30, 37, 38, 40, 63, 65, 83, 90, 92, 102, 107

an example of an "elite" college, 47-50
Europe, 2, 97
extra-curricular activity, 16, 22, 42, 43, 45, 49, 50, 57, 64, 72

Feuer, Lewis, 5, 13, 15
Forward Bloc, 118, 120
Free Press Journal, 162, 163

Gandhi, M. K. (Mahatma), 25, 59, 60, 61, 62, 66, 67, 68, 69, 71, 73, 75, 84, 89, 100, 106, 108, 109, 111, 113, 117, 120, 136, 184, 200
Gaudino, Robert, 36
Goa, 35, 146
Golwalkar, M. S., 152
Government Law College, 90
Grant Medical College, 93, 118
G. S. Medical College, 118
Gujarat State, 37, 52, 68
Gujaratis, 25, 29, 30, 78, 112, 138

Higher Education, 10, 11, 14, 20, 22, 24, 25, 71, 90, 98, 128 : in developing countries, 2; in India, 25, 26; relation of sexes in Indian, 27; Bombay as main center of, 28-29; in Bombay, 35-37, 37-54
Hind-Praja, 115, 188, 189
Hind Vidyarthi Sabha, 60
Hindu Mahasabha, 77

Indian Civil Service, 57
Indian Institute of Technology, Bombay, 29
Indian National Army, 126
Indian National Congress, 37, 57, 59, 60, 61, 62, 63, 66, 67, 69, 70, 71, 73, 75, 76, 77, 85, 87, 88, 89, 96, 97, 100, 101, 103, 104, 105, 113, 119, 120, 122, 123, 124, 185, 208; and the Naval Mutiny, 130-131; turns its back upon students, 132; changed attitude to students, 134; and Youth Congress, 138
Indian National Theatre, 104, 105, 109, 165
Indian Student News, 193
"Indiscipline", student, 11, 22, 136, 166, 169, 170
Institute of Science, 90
Isaacs, Harold, 42
Ismail Yusuf College, 107
Ivory Coast, 1

Jairazbhoy, A. Q., 179, 181
Jan Sangh, 151
Japan, 1, 5, 13, 19, 20, 203
Jinnah, M. A., 85, 174, 176, 177, 178
J. J. School of Art, 51
Joshi, P. C., 98, 104, 108
Joshi, P. M., 77
Joshi, S. M., 98, 144

Kanekar, Anant, 43
K. C. College, 38, 40
Khalsa College, 40, 41, 157
Korea, 1, 4, 20, 203
Kripalani, J. B., 122
Kripalani, Sucheta, 107
Kulkarni, Raja, 103
Kunte, Prabhakar, 136

Lajpat Rai, Lala, 60
Laski, Harold J., 67, 68
Leadership, Student, *see* Student Leadership
Lenin, 66, 67, 83
Lifton, Robert J., 7
Lipset, Seymour Martin, 4, 7
Lohia, Ram Manohar, 82, 98, 107
Lotvala, M., 186

Madras, 35, 69, 86, 87, 208
Maharashtra, 30, 36, 37, 47, 52, 58, 109, 146, 147, 149, 150

Maharashtrians, 25, 29, 78, 112, 138
Marathi Students' Association, 120
Marvick, Dwaine, 10
Marwari Youth League, 94
Marx, Karl, 66, 67, 68, 83, 109, 144
Marxism, 25, 67, 72, 83
Masani, M. R., 82, 86, 98
Matriculation examination, 90, 91, 92, 93, 128
McCully, Bruce, 26, 71
Medical Students' Union, 119
Meherally, Yusuf, 68, 77, 82, 144, 176
Mehta, Ashoka, 82, 98, 145, 189
Mehta, Pravina, 82, 103, 108, 110, 117
Mehta, Usha, 78, 146, 186
Merchant, Salim, 176, 177
Middle Ages, 2
mock parliaments, 165-166
"morning college" agitation, 157, 160, 200
Muslim League, 77, 78, 102, 114, 117, 119, 128, 174, 176, 178, 179, 180, 182
Muslim Students' Union, 64, 65, 94, 102, 119, 174-176, 177, 178, 179, 180, 181, 182, 183

Nagpur, 60, 87, 88, 148, 152
Namjoshi, A. N., 84, 159
Naoroji, Dadabhai, 57
Narayan, Jayaprakash, 144, 160, 189
Natarajan, S., 68
National Council of University Students of India, 193
National Discipline Scheme, 194
National Medical College, 60
National Student Press Council of India, 193
National Union of Students, 144, 160-164, 192
National Youth League, 75
Nationalist Volunteer League, 61
Naval mutiny, 113, 129-130
Nehru, Jawaharlal, 36, 68, 75, 85, 87, 111, 122, 160, 177

New Generation, 194
Non-cooperation Movement, 59, 61, 66, 149, 185
non-violence, 82, 88, 111
North Bombay Students' Union, 74, 103, 115

Organizations, student, *see* student organizations

Pakistan, 128, 174, 176, 179, 180, 190
Parikh, G. D., 158, 159
Parsi community, 25, 29, 30, 78
Parsi Students' Association, 64
Patel, Vallabhbhai, 120
Patil, S. K., 62
Peoples' Education Society, 40, 41
Peoples' Theatre, 64, 101, 105, 165
Phansekar, Arvind, 160
Phatak, N. R., 58, 103
Podar College, 41
Poland, 7
Political activity, of students, 10-14, 74-84
Political Sufferers Relief Fund, 119
Poonja, Vaman, 141, 142, 143
Pradhan, Vijay, 145, 146
Progressive Group, 75

"Quit India" movement, 73, 100-112, 113, 200

Ranade, M. G., 47
Rashtra Seva Dal, 119, 146-148, 167
Rashtriya Swayamsevak Sangh (R.S.S.), 76, 77, 95, 102, 114, 117, 148-153, 206
Rasputin Group, 63
Redkar, P., 143
Revolutionary Socialist Party, 118, 120
R. L. Trust Hostel, 95-96
Round Table Conferences, 78

Roy, M. N., 83
Royal Indian Navy, 130
Ruia College, 41, 188
Russian Revolution, 83, 84

Sakrikar, D., 57, 60, 62, 63, 85, 86, 187, 192
Samajwadi Yuvak Sabha, 145, 146
Sanghvi, Ramesh, 96
Sathi, 189
Satyagraha, 89
Scheduled Caste (Untouchables) Students' Federation, 78
Secondary School Certificate Examination (S.S.C.), 29, 33, 156
Sethna, M., 139
Shah, M. L., 78
Shallat, Dr., 161
Shils, Edward, 7
Siddharth College, 38, 39, 49, 166; an example of a "new" college, 41-47
Sikh Students' Federation, 78
Simon Commission, 61, 62
Sinha, Ramakrishna, 122
Smelser, Neil, 12, 27
S. N. D. T. Women's University, 37, 52-53, 152
Soares, Glaucio A. D., 4, 28, 207
social action, of students, 7, 8, 10, 11
Socialist Party of India, 144, 145
Socialist Student Movement, 144-148
South Indian Education Society's College, 40
Soviet Union, 83, 85, 88, 101, 115
Spanish Civil War, 97
Spencer, Metta, 3, 24, 207
Srinivas, M. N., 26
St. Xavier's College, 30, 38, 40, 63, 65, 90, 102, 163, 165, 166
St. Xavier's Institute of Education, 53
Student activity, 10-14, 22, 27, 89-96
Student attitudes, 22
Student leadership, 26-27, 169, 202-203, 206-207

Student movement(s), 1, 3, 4, 5, 6, 9, 11, 14-18, 19, 20, 21, 22: norm-oriented, 12-13; value-oriented, 12-13; definition, 14-15; leadership of, 26; roots of, in Bombay, 57-72; politicization of, in Bombay, 73-99; and 1942 movement in Bombay, 100-112; and independence, 113-133; since 1947, in Bombay, 134-170; response to change in society, 134-136; communist, 139-143; socialist, 144-148; right-wing, 148-153; transition in Bombay, 196-211
student organization(s), 14-18, 19-20, 21, 22, 23, 26, 70, 72, 73, 80, 93, 96, 97, 99, 114, 117, 196, 198-200, 201, 202, 203-206: "official", 15; extra-curricular, 16, 22; unapproved, 16-17; educational role of, 18-20; effect of political condition on, 24-25; effect of economic situation on, 25; different types and emphases of, 27-28; and "Quit India" movement, 102-108; communal, 173-183
Student Press in India, 184-195; the nationalist, 185-189; the communist, 189-191; since independence, 191-195
Student, The, 104, 121, 126, 129, 150, 188, 190, 191
"Student Unity Manifesto", 116
Student(s): increasing importance, 1-2; characteristics of, in developing countries, 2-6; pressures on, 6-10; aspects of their political activity, 10-14; movements and organizations, 14-18; activity, 22; background of Indian, 23; environment in India, 22-54; roots of their movement in Bombay, 57-72; politicization of their movement in Bombay, 73-99; and "Quit India" movement, 100-112; in prison, 108-109; and Independence, 113-133; and politics since 1947, 134-170; press in India, 184-195

Students' Anti-Untouchable Committee, 62-63
Students' Brotherhood, 62, 63, 64-67, 68, 71, 72, 79, 91
Students' Brotherhood Quarterly, 64, 185
Students' Call, The, 186, 187
Students' Chronicle, 193
Students' Digest, 192, 193
Students' Federation, The, 187
Students' Tribune, The, 187
Students' Unity Committee, 115, 116, 117, 124
Students' Unity Conference (August 1943), 115-116
Swatantra Party, 66, 86
Sydenham College, 118

Tata Institute for Fundamental Research, 35
Tata Institute of Social Science, 35
Tilak, B. G., 47, 58, 148, 152
Times of India, 107
Trillin, Calvin, 16
Turkey, 1, 20, 59

United States, 5, 16, 97
University News, 192
University of Bombay, 24, 28, 35-37, 38, 39, 47, 51, 52, 65, 91, 92, 105, 110, 121, 157, 158, 159
University of London, 35

University Reform League, 94, 95
Untouchables, 63, 125

Varde, S. S., 147
Varma, Ravindra, 123
Victoria Jubilee Technical Institute, 90, 105, 154-155
Vidyarthi Parishad, 44, 150-153, 206
Vivekananda, Swami, 148, 152

Wadia, Professor P. A., 118
Wales, Prince of, 58
Webb, Sidney, 67, 68
West African Students' Union, 20
Wilson College, 30, 38, 40, 58, 60, 63, 65, 77, 107, 118, 188
World War II, 67, 84, 100, 132, 140, 187

Young India, 184, 185
Young India League, 58
Young Liberator, 185
Young Men's Hindu Association, 64, 94, 120
Young Men's Parsi Association, 94, 120
Youth, 194
Youth Congress, 137, 138, 139, 193, 194

Zengakuren, 1, 13, 19